A TEA BAG
IN A
HOT WATER
WORLD

A TEA BAG
IN A
HOT WATER WORLD

TREMELL J. COLLINS SR.

PR MIX
PUBLISHING
THE WRITE CHOICE

Primix Publishing
East Brunswick Office Evolution
1 Tower Center Boulevard, Ste 1510
East Brunswick, NJ 08816
www.primixpublishing.com
Phone: 1-800-538-5788

Published by Primix Publishing: 08/11/2025

ISBN: 979-8-89194-513-5(sc)
ISBN: 979-8-89194-514-2(hc)
ISBN: 979-8-89194-515-9(e)

Library of Congress Control Number: 2025912006

Any people depicted in stock imagery provided by iStock are models, and such images are being used for illustrative purposes only.

Certain stock imagery © iStock.

A TEA BAG IN A HOT WATER WORLD

TREMELL'S THE first to say he doesn't have it together. No one has it together? With the personal stories and solid biblical teaching that open your heart to God's truth. Tremell guild you to a deeper faith and exuberant desire to follow the Lord though life's most turbulent storm's. open your eyes to see the full wholeness God has for you.

AUTHOR

TREMELL J COLLINS SR.

A Tea Bag In A Hot Water World

ACKNOWLEDGEMENTS

I acknowledge those individuals who have given me suggestions and thoughts and helped me compile and put together this book. bobby jean Williams, Bob Peterson, Michelle Vestal, Ben Maxwell, to all my Sons Tyrelle, Tremell Jr, Travon and all my family members I love you all. Those who criticized mocked and did not believe in the book I thank you. You kept me on my Knees you kept me desperate for God to do the Impossible you kept me on my Determined to do thus said The Lord... Grateful acknowledgements is given to numerous contributions throughout my life and Ministry mentioned and UN mentioned who have poured into me shared me, and believed in the call of God in my life...

THE GOD OF THE JOURNEY

ON his journey, Abraham took the linear view. He knew he was going somewhere, and though he was not able to see the end of time, he was able to see the one who owns all time, God Almighty. Being a journeyer in the tradition of Abraham means having our eyes on the God of the journey we can rest in the knowledge that the God of the universe, our loving Father, is the one who determines where we're going and how fast we'll get there. It all comes down to how we view our journey and how we view ourselves in the midst of it. this is such a difficult issue for so many of us. If we don't understand that our life is a journey and that journeys by their very nature have ups and downs, starts and stops, days of sunshine and days of rain, we'll lose hope, both for ourselves and for others. God will continue to lead us on that linear road to perfection. In a world full of toxic relationships, crippled values and mutilated morality, lives our crying out for a real change not Band-Aids, not being drug-induced solutions Mend broken hearts and RESTORIES SHATTERED LIVES A TEA BAG IN A HOT WATER WORLD...

FORWARD

When Tremell Collins announces his plans for his book in our conversation on the phone I did not realize the Magnitude of the job he took on with such Verse. I have been instructed and rewarded watching Tremell unfold this book. This book is not only good read for Life but a fine book for all people....

COPY WRITER TREMELL J. COLLINS

ACKNOWLEDGEMENTS #2

Tremell

It was amazing meeting with you today! I can tell you that you are very strong in your faith. And I learned a lot. I loved your Tea. Thank for the conversation, you're in my prayers!

Kahe

Tremell

It was such an honor to meet you, your words and stories really inspired me and my faith. It seems that you have created a strong relationship with our God and that was so incredible to see. Thank you so much for helping me with my faith. You're in my prayers!

-Sarah

Tremell

This is how God showed his love for us 1 John3:16 and we ought to lay down our lives for our brothers and sisters.

Kenelall E.
Redmond, WA

Love God you will change the world. We preach the Gospel to the ends of the world, and we will not falter. It was a Blessing to meet you may God go with you to the ends of the world in Jesus Christ's name, don't back down, don't give up.

Jordan

Bellevue, WA

Tremell

I'm really blessed by talking to you; you show me how amazing God is and God's grace. Thank you for telling mee that everyone is special. I will pray that my Holy Spirit to talk to God and ask him for help. Thank you for strengthen my Faith in God.

_Qi Zhu (Kath erne) from U.W., Originally from China Beijing.

Tremell

Thanks you for visiting us here at our Church! May your Ministry flourish & reach out many souls that need Jesus! I would always remember not to stay in the salt shaker! But be salt in this World! Those are very good stuff! Continue to be a light in this World!

In Christ

Richmond D

Hope of the City Church

Tremell

Being drug free is wonderful especially when you can live it! not just because of how you are and will become!

-Chota

Tremell

Until man has found God and God has found him. He begins at no beginning words towards no end!

-Lance Alexander

Tremell

My name is Sandy and we met in Seattle at a July 30th Sea Fair Parade life's journey is always complicated and your message to keep it Simple, Pursue your dreams, keep strong and look out for each other is really Important!

God Bless!

-Sandy

Just met Tremell this day 9/15/2011 at Union Station What a humble Man of God I dearly enjoyed being here with him & Learn a lot about Life itself through Jesus Christ!

-Douglass

So cool to hear what God has done through you. I only have been trying to follow God for less than a year and can learn a lot from you. It's so true that the Church is not a place to meet in a building only on Sunday will see you again Awesome to meet a Brother!

-Ben

Listening to what God is doing in your life is Amazing. Continue to build your Treasures in heaven.

God is always with you for sharing your story. Continue to do his will

Much Love!

-Brian Kim

I've been spiritually lost all my life until this year 2011. I found myself being spiritually pulled in every direction in the current Church I am involved in M.C. Like what you said, Tremell It's all about having character and influence. We live in a world where people are intimately selfish. Being able to find the importance in loving one other regardless of who they are or where they are from is something I learned during my growth God has provoked me to push myself even further. And I am grateful for him bring light in my life so that I can spread it to others. Thank you. Tremell.

-George Lee

Tremell you are a wise man. I know that God is going to have so many Great plans for you. Continue playing your part in God's Great Symphony! Surely the Treasures of Heaven will be shown to you.

-Chris

I pray that your Ministry grows and that you stay Strong!

-Michael B

It's so nice to know that there's someone out here doing God's work. keep up the good work. I'll be praying that you will change other's lives being out here.

-Heather Chan

I am so happy to meet you today. It has opened up my eyes to another side of society. Keep up the good work.

-Sund Cheng

Life isn't about running from the storm. It's about leaning in the rain."

-Cindy

The person who says it can e done, is being passed by the person who is doing it!

-Sarah

"For all we know we only get One chance at One Lifetime, If this is true you need to think, Do you want the One possible Life chance remember as a hard, miserable, disappointing night mare or do you want your memory to linger with as many as you can! Live Life as if you only have one chance to Live it!

-Mary Jayne. Quinn

Tremell
Keep doing what you do spending your time trying to help those in need. A willingness to listen and help is all some of the people you meet need.

-Dyna

Nice talking to you thanks for being (Genuine)
Stand up for Kids"
-Anastasia

The hope of your heart is open to interpretation of
how you see the world through the eyes of the world.
But when you see the world through God's eyes you
have a heart for people, when you pour your heart out
to the people you are giving Gods words and filling the
people with God's Love.
Michelle Henry

We are here because there is no refuge from ourselves
until a person confront himself, through the eyes of
others he will be alone.
-john Scott

Proverbs 24;16 For a righteous man falls seven
times and rises again But the wicked stumble in time
of calamity.
-Cristal

Tremell
May the Lord continue to bless you and your Passion
for Jesus Christ? Continue to "Run To Win" for the
Lord-1 cor. 9:24-27.
Mike Rohrbach, Director
Run to Win Outreach, www. Run To Win. Org

CONTENTS

MY JOURNEY #1

I DEDICATE THE CONTENTS OF THIS WORK TO MY CHILDREN, **TYRELLE J. COLLINS, TREMELL J. COLLINS JR., TRAVON B. COLLINS** MY PROTECTOR, PROVIDER AND ALL THAT JESUS CHRIST LORD. I PRESENT every word back to you as you have given them to me. I give you back THE ministry you gave to me. I love you lord and I thank you for opening the eyes of my understanding so that I would know the hope of the calling. I would like to declare that I am nothing without you. I gave all the honor, glory and praise for helping me with this project. Praise the Lord by God's grace and mercy he has anointed me to release the information in this book to his body my journey begin in 1983 in CT. at the **Mount Olive Baptist Church.** I SERVED THERE AS A **SUNDAY SCHOOL TEACHER AND ALSO SERVED AS A DEACON FOR A NUMBER OF YEARS. I served as the president of the Conn Baptist Deacons Alliance, I also served as the Fourth vice president of the national Baptist deacon's Convention of America. I got Ordained in 2006 as a ELDER the service was great and the spirit was present** the people at the service was awesome God used me minister the word of God from the book of Jude. The song that was played **Yes by Shekinah Glory** was so powerful to send me off in the ministry. Also a song by **William Murphy LIKE NEVER BEFORE** was standout songs still to today they ring in my ears. To GOD be the GLORY.. I moved to SEATTLE, WASHINGTON IN 2008 after I got married I it ended in 2010. I learned a lesson in being in God's will and staying the course later God showed. Me I was like **tea bag in a Hot water world.** I felt like a tea bag in Hot water waiting for the release of what God desposited in me. I AM THANKFUL to GOD that he is faithful he allowed me to go thru. I woke up 5:30a.m had prayer asked God to give me direction and lead me to give a word that would help someone I needed God to show up confirm what he said to me to use men and this morning me **Troy, Rick, Jason, Francis and Leroy** walked out the bread of life mission and walked a crossed the street to read THE Seattle Times headlines of the day then we had a discussion about things that were happening in each other's lives the topic Dysfunctional FAMILYS God showed me on Sunday through the word in Genises chapters 12-50 the dysfunction we men have to take the lead. AMERICA is #1 in family dysfunction God showed that I have to get myself right with him being intimate spending tome with GOD. Getting breast milk from God. God to give me a fresh revelation. Our talk was enlighting **JASON** THE YOUNGEST SOME POINT ABOUT TRIGGERING our emotions the soulish area and not just the spirit it needs to be a balance and how the church world has not effectively dealt with it. **Troy** shared with us about the fruit of the spirit and **Francis** shared about he is growing by being around me and Troy. And having patience with his wife, I talked about daring to be a man and being penalty box lessons from Moses and I went to the train station to finishing journaling God is good. **<u>HOLY DISCIPLINED TO BE DIFFERENT</u>**

STRETSCH IT'S Within reach disciplined to be different as God's chosen people the Israelites were commanded to be holy exodus 22:31 to be consecrated means to be separated this is Christian Life Style should be different and separated from the rest of the world. We obtain holiness through a disciplined and determined pursuit of God. We must correct mold and train ourselves in the word of God because it is by willing, prayerful and persistent obedience to requirements of scriptures that godly patterns are developed and become a part of us. Learning the word of God will bring this word to your heart and mind as you make decisions in keeping with His will and character only when we do this in a persistent way that we find the holiness that reflects his character be empowered through the word of God read it day and night memorize it Psalms119:11 God has destined us to be conformed to the image of Jesus Christ our transformation is always at work through Jesus and the Holy Spirit nurtures us in our spiritual development makes it your business to be holy every day. **Dear Lord** help me to pursue holiness everyday help take hold of Christ's Strength every day. Help me **overcome challenges** every day. Help me to **defeat obstacles** every day. God is the great God of reversal he takes what is Overwhelming to me and uses it to give me **Victory...**

MY JOURNEY ELDER TREMELL J. COLLINS

WE all begin our lives as empty note books every day we have an opportunity to record new experiences on our pages with the turning of each we gain more knowledge and understanding ideally as we progress our note book our notebook becomes filled with notation and observations the problem is that not all people make the best use of their notebook closed most of their lives they rarely jot down anything at all others fill their pages but they never take time to reflect on them and gain greater wisdom and understanding but few not only make a record of what they experience they linger over it and ponder it's meaning they reread what is written and reflection turns experience into insight so they not only live the experience but learn from it they understand time is on their side if they use their notebook as a calendar they come to understand a secret experience teaches nothing but evaluated experience teaches everything you know there is a parable of a fox, wolf, and a bear one day they went hunting together after each of them caught a deer they discuss how to divide the spoils the bear asked the wolf how he thought it should be done the wolf said everyone should get one deer suddenly the bear ate the wolf. Then the bear asked the fox how he proposed to divide things up the fox offered the bear his deer and then said the bear ought take the wolf deer as well. Where did you get such wisdom asked the bear from the wolf replied the fox... Oliver Wendell Holmes said the young man knows the rules but the old man knows the exceptions when taking time to evaluate his experience. Experience is not the best Teacher

Experience teaches nothing but evaluated experience teaches everything.

1. WE all experience more than we understand.
2. Our attitude towards unplanned and unpleasant experiences determines our growth.
3. Lack of experience is costly.
4. Experience is costly.
5. Not evaluating and learning from experience is more costly.
6. Evaluated experience lifts a person above the crowd people who make it regular practice. To reflect on their experiences evaluate what went wrong and right and learn from them are rare but when you meet one you know it.

MYJOURNEY ELDER TREMELLJ. COLLINS

WE all begin our lives as empty note books every day we have an opportunity to record new experiences on our pages with the turning of each we gain more knowledge and understanding ideally as we progress our note book our notebook becomes filled with notation and observations the problem is that not all people make the best use of their notebook closed most of their lives they rarely jot down anything at all others fill their pages but they never take time to reflect on them and gain greater wisdom and understanding but few not only make a record of what they experience they linger over it and ponder it's meaning they reread what is written and reflection turns experience into insight so they not only live the experience but learn from it they understand time is on their side if they use their notebook as a calendar they come to understand a secret experience teaches nothing but evaluated experience teaches everything you know there is a parable of a fox, wolf, and a bear one day they went hunting together after each of them caught a deer they discuss how to divide the spoils the bear asked the wolf how he thought it should be done the wolf said everyone should get one deer suddenly the bear ate the wolf. Then the bear asked the fox how he proposed to divide things up the fox offered the bear his deer and then said the bear ought take the wolf deer as well. Where did you get such wisdom asked the bear from the wolf replied the fox... Oliver Wendell Holmes said the young man knows the rules but the old man knows the exceptions when taking time to evaluate his experience. Experience is not the best Teacher

Experience teaches nothing but evaluated experience teaches everything.

1. WE all experience more than we understand.
2. Our attitude towards unplanned and unpleasant experiences determines our growth.
3. Lack of experience is costly.
4. Experience is costly.

5. Not evaluating and learning from experience is more costly.

6. Evaluated experience lifts a person above the crowd people who make it regular practice. To reflect on their experiences evaluate what went wrong and right and learn from them are rare but when you meet one you know it.

TEA BAG IN A HOT WATER WORLD #1

THERE are two ways to drink TEA. Some people are dippers. They dip their tea bag up and down in the mug. A lot of people are like that. They dip in on Sunday morning then dip back out. They dip back in on Wednesday night then they dip back out. But there's another way to drink tea. And that's to be abiding. That involves the act of just dropping the bag in the water and letting it stay there. Without touching the bag amazing thing happen the color of the water begins to change as the influence of the bag in hot water effects change in the cup. A person can just sit and watch the transformation take place because of the act of abiding when you are a dipper you've got to make things happen by your own effort. You've got to move the bag up and down, A spoon in and out of the cup, wrap the string around the spoon, jerk, and then pull. It can require a human effort. But when you are abiding. The water changes all by itself. Once I was meeting with a guy and we were both drinking tea. He was dipping and pulling away. I just let my bag sit. He told me that he couldn't let is tea bag sit in the water like that because his would get to strong. That's exactly what happens when you abiding will determine the rate of your progress in the Spiritual Life. Jesus wants you to stay there and experience the Full Strength of his Presence. Taken from a book I really love "Tony Evans Book of "ILLustrations". About a Tea Bag are lives are sometimes like a tea bag. So is my journey and so is yours. **A Tea Bag Journey**. The inward Journey involves us in an ever deeping, **Authentic engagement with self, with God and with others.** **The inward Journey Taken Seriously** leads to the discovery of the outward: The place our gifts and Brokenness connect with a need in the world. To much Time in a Spiritual Rest Stop results in Stagnation missed Opportunities, Pride, Blindness and loss of zeal Rev3:16 good or bad, God call's us to be Pioneers, not Settlers.

MY JOURNEY #1

I DEDICATE THE CONTENTS OF THIS WORK
TO MY CHILDERN, **TYRELLE J. COLLINS,
TREMELL J. COLLINS JR., TRAVON B. COLLINS**
MY PROTECTOR, PROVIDER AND ALL THAT
JESUS CHRIST LORD.I PRESENT every word back
to you as you have given them to me. I give you back
THE ministry you gave to me. I love you lord and I
thank you for opening the eyes of my understanding
so that I would know the hope of the calling. I would
like to declare that I am nothing without you. I gave
all the honor, glory and praise for helping me with this
project. Praise the Lord by God's grace and mercy he

has anointed me to release the information in this book to his body my journey begin in 1983 in CT .at the **Mount Olive Baptist Church**. I SERVED THERE AS **A SUNDAY SCHOOL TEACHER AND ALSO SERVED AS A DEACON FOR A NUMBER OF YEARS. I served as the president of the Conn Baptist Deacons Alliance, I also served as the Fourth vice president of the national Baptist deacon's Convention of America. I got Ordained in 2006 as a ELDER the service was great and the spirit was present** the people at the service was awesome God used me minister the word of God from the book of Jude. The song that was played **Yes by Shekinah Glory** was so powerful to send me off in the ministry. Also a song by **William Murphy LIKE NEVER BEFORE** was standout songs still to today they ring in my ears. To GOD be the GLORY. I moved to SEATTLE, WASHINGTON in 2008 after I got married I it ended in 2010. I learned a lesson in being in God's will and staying the course later God showed. Me I was like a **tea bag in a Hot water world**. I felt like a tea bag in Hot water waiting for the release of what God deposited in me. I AM THANKFUL to GOD that he is faithful he allowed me to go thru. I woke up 5:30a.m had prayer asked god to give me direction and lead me to give a word that would help someone I needed God to show up confirm what he said to me to use what I have in my hands, and to minister the word to some men and this morning me **Troy, Rick, Jason, FRANCIS and Leroy** walked out the bread of life mission and walked a crossed the street to read

THE Seattle Times headlines of the day then we had a discussion about things that were happening in each other's lives the topic Dysfunctional FAMILYS God showed me on Sunday through the word in Genises chapters 12-50 the dysfunction we men have to take the lead. AMERICA is #1 in family dysfunction God showed that I have to get myself right with him being intimate spending time with God. Getting the breast milk from God. God to give me a fresh revelation. Our talk was enlighting **JASON** THE YOUNGEST HAD SOME GOOD POINTS ABOUT TRIGGERING our emotions by others and we talk to him on how we need to deal with our emotions the soulish area and not just the spirit it needs to be a balance and how the church world has not effectively dealt with it. **Troy** shared with us about the fruit of the spirit and **Francis** shared about how he is growing by being around me and Troy. And having patience with his wife talked about daring to be a man and being in the penalty box lessons from Moses and I went to the train station to finishing journaling God is good. **HOLY DISCIPLINED TO BE DIFFERENT**

STRETCH IT'S Within reach disciplined to be different as God's chosen people the Israelites were commanded to be holy exodus 22:31 to be holy means to be different to be consecrated means to be separated this is Christian Life Style should be different and separated from the rest of the world. We obtain holiness through a disciplined and determined pursuit of God. We must correct mold and train ourselves in the word of God because it is by willing, prayerful and persistent obedience to requirements of scriptures that godly patterns are developed and become a part of us. Learning the word of God will bring this word to your heart and mind as you make decisions in keeping with His will and character only when we do this in a persistent way that we find the holiness that reflects his character be empowered through the word of God read it day and night memorize it Psalms119:11 God has destined us to be conformed to the image of Jesus Christ our transformation is always at work through Jesus and the Holy Spirit nurtures us in our spiritual development makes it your business to be holy every day. **Dear Lord** help me to pursue holiness everyday help take hold of Christ's Strength every day. Help me **overcome challenges** every day. Help me to **defeat obstacles** every day. God is the great God of reversal he takes what is Overwhelming to me and uses it to give me **Victory...**

MY JOURNEY ELDER TREMELL J. COLLINS

WE all begin our lives as empty note books every day we have an opportunity to record new experiences on our pages with the turning of each we gain more knowledge and understanding ideally as we progress our note book our notebook becomes filled with notation and observations the problem is that not all people make the best use of their notebook closed most of their lives they rarely jot down anything at all others fill their pages but they never take time to reflect on them and gain greater wisdom and understanding but few not only make a record of what they experience they linger over it and ponder it's meaning they reread what is written and reflection turns experience into insight so they not only live the experience but learn from it they understand time is on their side if they use their notebook as a calendar they come to understand a secret experience teaches nothing but evaluated experience teaches everything you know there is a parable of a fox ,wolf, and a bear one day they went hunting together after each of them caught a deer they discuss how to divide the spoils the bear asked the wolf how he thought it should be done the wolf said everyone should get one deer suddenly the bear ate the wolf. Then the bear asked the fox how he proposed to divide things up the fox offered the bear his deer and then said the bear ought take the wolf deer as well. Where did you get such wisdom asked the bear from the wolf replied the fox... Oliver Wendell Holmes said the young man knows the rules but the old man knows the exceptions when taking time to evaluate his experience. Experience is not the best Teacher

Experience teaches nothing but evaluated experience teaches everything.

1. WE all experience more than we understand.
2. Our attitude towards unplanned and unpleasant experiences determines our growth.

3. Lack of experience is costly.
4. Experience is costly.
5. Not evaluating and learning from experience is more costly.
6. Evaluated experience lifts a person above the crowd people who make it regular practice. To reflect on their experiences evaluate what went wrong and right and learn from them are rare but when you meet one you know it.

MYJOURNEY ELDER TREMELLJ. COLLINS

WE all begin our lives as empty note books every day we have an opportunity to record new experiences on our pages with the turning of each we gain more knowledge and understanding ideally as we progress our note book our notebook becomes filled with notation and observations the problem is that not all people make the best use of their notebook closed most of their lives they rarely jot down anything at all others fill their pages but they never take time to reflect on them and gain greater wisdom and understanding but few not only make a record of what they experience they linger over it and ponder it's meaning they reread what is written and reflection turns experience into insight so they not only live the experience but learn from it they understand time is on their side if they use their notebook as a calendar they come to understand a secret experience teaches nothing but evaluated experience teaches everything you know there is a parable of a fox ,wolf, and a bear one day they went hunting together after each of them caught a deer they discuss how to divide the spoils the bear asked the wolf how he thought it should be done the wolf said everyone should get one deer suddenly the bear ate the wolf. Then the bear asked the fox how he proposed to divide things up the fox offered the bear his deer and then said the bear ought take the wolf deer as well. Where did you get such wisdom asked the bear from the wolf replied the fox... Oliver Wendell Holmes said the young man knows the rules but the old man knows the exceptions when taking time to evaluate his experience. Experience is not the best Teacher

Experience teaches nothing but evaluated experience teaches everything.

1. WE all experience more than we understand.
2. Our attitude towards unplanned and unpleasant experiences determines our growth.

3. Lack of experience is costly.
4. Experience is costly.
5. Not evaluating and learning from experience is more costly.
6. Evaluated experience lifts a person above the crowd people who make it regular practice. To reflect on their experiences evaluate what went wrong and right and learn from them are rare but when you meet one you know it.

TEA BAG INA HOT WATER WORLD #1

THERE are two ways to drink TEA. Some people are dippers. They dip their tea bag up and down in the mug. A lot of people are like that. They dip in on Sunday morning then dip back out. They dip back in on Wednesday night then they dip back out. But there's another way to drink tea. And that's to be abiding. That involves the act of just dropping the bag in the water and letting it stay there. Without touching the bag amazing thing happen the color of the water begins to change as the influence of the bag in hot water effects change in the cup. A person can just sit and watch the Transformation take place because of the act of abiding when you are a dipper you've got to make things happen by your own effort. You've got to move the bag up and down, A spoon in and out of the cup, wrap the string around the spoon, jerk, and then pull. It can require a human effort. But when you are abiding. The water changes all by itself. Once I was meeting with a guy and we were both drinking tea. He was dipping and pulling away. I just let my bag sit. He told me that he couldn't let his tea bag sit in the water like that because his would get too strong. That's exactly what happens when you abiding will determine the rate of your progress in the Spiritual Life. Jesus wants you to stay there and experience the Full Strength of his Presence. Taken from a book I really love "Tony Evans Book of "1LLustrations". About a Tea Bag are lives are sometimes like a tea bag. So, is my journey and so is yours. **A Tea Bag Journey**. The inward Journey involves us in an ever deeping, **Authentic engagement with self, with God and with others**. **The inward Journey Taken Seriously** leads to the discovery of the outward: The place our gifts and Brokenness connect with a need in the world. Too much Time in a Spiritual Rest Stop results in Stagnation missed Opportunities, Pride, Blindness and loss of zeal Rev3:16 good or bad, God call's us to be Pioneers, not Settlers.

A TEA BAG EXPERIENCE MEN AND THEIR WIVES

One Day at a conference in Dallas, TX I heard Dr. Tony Evans speak on men and their wives. He said I don't know if you've seen one but there are square watermelons now. Of course people are trying to figure out how making a square watermelon is possible. Normally the fruit is **OBlong** but somebody somewhere decided to try growing a watermelon in a square container. The idea was to control the size of the watermelon so it can easily sit in the refrigerator. They force the watermelon to readjust from its natural tendency to become **OBLONG** to a new shape determined by the environment if a man feels like he's got an oblong wife who's going in the wrong direction, Maybe the environment she's going in doesn't allow her to change her natural shape. A husband has the power to set the tone and change the environment. I've learned that lesson. It was a powerful one on Tea Bag Experience in marriage, Spiritual Transformation. Rom 12:2 Eph 5:25-33)

A long marriage is two people trying to dance a duet and two solos at the same time. ANNE TAYLOR, FLEMING"

Each personality brings a combination of strengths and weaknesses to the relationship.

A TEA BAG EXPERIENCE
INA HOT WATER WORLD

2 CORINTHIANS 12:17-12:10

2 Corinthians 12:7 Because of the surpassing greatness of the revelations, for this reason, to keep me from exalting myself, there was given me a thorn in the flesh, a messenger of Satan to torment me to keep me from exalting myself! 8 Concerning this I implored the lord three times that it might leave me .9 And he has

said to me," My grace is sufficient for you, for power is perfected in weakness." Most gladly, therefore I will rather boast about my weaknesses, so that the power of Christ may dwell in me.10 Therefore I am content with weaknesses, with distresses, with persecutions, with difficulties, for Christ sake: for when I am weak, then I am strong.

A tea bag experience in a hot water world!

Thesis: The thing in life that causes you the most pain can be your greatest gift from God! December 23, 2009

The Lord knows how to balance our lives. If we only have blessing, we may become proud: So he permits us to have burdens as well. Paul's great experience in heaven could have ruined his ministry on earth: so God, in his goodness, permitted Satan to buffet Paul in order to keep him from becoming proud. The mystery of human suffering will not be solved completely in this life. Sometimes we suffer simply because we are humans. Our bodies change as we grow older, and we are susceptible to the normal problems of life. The same body that can bring us pleasures can also bring us pains. The same family members and friends that delight us can also break our hearts. This is a part of the "human comedy" And the only way to escape it is to be less than human. But nobody wants to take that route. Sometimes we suffer because we are foolish and disobedient to the lord. Our own rebellion may afflict us, or the lord may see fit to chasten us in his love (heb.12:3). King David suffered greatly because of his sin: the consequences were painful and so was the discipline of God (see 2 Sam 12:1-22:Ps. 51) IN his grace, God forgive our sins: but in his government, he permits us to reap what we Sow. Suffering also is a tool God uses for building character (rom.5:1-5). Certainly Paul was a man of rich Christian character because he permitted God to mold and make him in the painful experiences of life. When you walk along the shore of the ocean, you notice that the rocks are sharp in the quiet coves, but polished in those places where the waves beat against them. God can use the" waves and billows" of life to polish us, if we will let him. Paul's thorn in the flesh was given to him to keep him from sinning. Exciting spiritual experiences- like going to heaven and back- have a way of inflating the human ego: and pride leads to multitude of temptations to sin. Had Paul's heart been filled with pride, those next fourteen years would have been filled with failure instead of success. We do not know what the thorn in the flesh was. The word translated thorn means 'la sharp stake used for torturing or impaling someone. "It was physical affliction of some kind that brought pain and distress to Paul. God permitted Satan to afflict Paul, just as he permitted Satan to afflict Job (see Jobl-2) While we do not fully understand the origin of evil in this universe, or all the purposes God had in mind when he permitted evil to come, we do not know that God controls evil and can use it even for his own glory. Satan cannot work against a believer without the permission of God. Everything that the enemy did to Job and Paul was permitted by the will of God. When God permits suffering to come to our lives, there are several ways we can deal with it. Some people become bitter and blame God for robbing them of freedom and pleasure. Others just "give up" and fail to get any blessing out of the experience because they will not put any courage into experience. Still others grit their teeth and put on a brave front, determined to "endure to the very end. "While this is courageous response, it usually drains them of the strength needed for daily living: and after time, they may collapse. Two messages were involved in this painful experience. The thorn in the flesh was Satan's message to Paul, but God had another message for Him, a message of grace. The tense verb in 2 corinthians12:9 is Important: "and He {God} has once —for all said to me."" God gave Paul a message that stayed with him. The words Paul heard while he was in heaven, he was not permitted to share with us: But he did share the words God gave him on earth — and what an encouragement they are. It was a message of grace. What is grace? It is God's provision for our every need when we need it. God's riches at Christ's Expense. It was a message of sufficient grace. There is never a shortage of grace. God is sufficient for our spiritual needs. In the Christian life we get many blessings through transformation, not substitution. When Paul prayed three times for the removal of his pain, he was asking God for a substitution: give me health instead of sickness, deliverance instead of pain and weakness. "Sometimes God does meet the need by substitution: But other times He meets the need by transformation. He does not remove the affliction, but he gives us his grace so that the affliction works for us and not against us. As Paul Prayed about his problem, God gave him deeper insight into what He was doing. Paul learned that his thorn in the flesh was a gift from God. What a strange gift! There was only one thing for Paul to do: accept the gift from God and allow God to accomplish his purposes. God wanted to keep Paul from being "exalted above measure," and this is his way of accomplishing it. What is God trying to keep you from doing? Or becoming? From Paul's experience, we may learn several practical lessons.

1. The spiritual is more important to believer than the physical. This is not to suggest that we ignore the physical, because our bodies are the temples of God. But it does mean that we try not to make our bodies an end in themselves. They are Gods tools for accomplishing his work in this world. What God does in developing our Christian character is far more valuable than the physical healing without character.

2. God knows how to balance burdens and Blessing, Suffering and glory. Life is something like a prescription: the individual ingredients might hurt us, but when properly blended, they help us.

3. Not all sickness is cause by sin. The argument of Job's comforters was that he

had sinned, that was why he was suffering. But their argument was wrong in Job's case, as well as in Paul's case. There are times when God permits Satan to afflict us so that God might accomplish a great purpose in our lives.

4. We can always rest in God's word. He always has a message of encouragement for us in times of trial and suffering. Paul knew about that Power, because he trusted the will of God and depended on the grace of God. That same power can be ours today. **My strength comes into its own in your weakness.**

LIFE'S JOURNEY

As we go about life's journeys finding time to celebrate is inevitable to be able to praise the lord with music song and dance is an expression of art that should inspire us to celebrate the coming of the lord. The presence of the lord, and the spirit of the lord Holy in my walk. Someone plan a walk for a worthy cause they ask for money to sponsor them they take the walk but so too in our daily journey with God we work so that others may get the benefit by our intercession by prayer by holy example. But not everyone could take this walk. The invitation is limited to a select few only those with pure motives and guiltless actions can have access to God would you be able to take this walk if not ask God to examine today my motives and actions. God thank you for Jesus power to cleanse and to lift me. I need your guidance to help others to believe that they do can walk to and stand in holy places with you let it be by my walk others will come to Front Line Ministries. What must I do to be saved? Also I met a security guard and talked about marriage and my journey here to Seattle and God is transforming me into his image Praise God. God has selected me as his treasured possession. We are forever worth more to God than anything we can imagine. We are sealed as his priceless inheritance he made us in his image and called me to be Extraordinary. We are gifts to God from God. God has hidden us in his heart where his treasure reside. Love for God demonstrated in obedience, our joy in the Lord that honor's him with thanksgiving and peace in the Lord that produces patience. And without faith we give up on God's purpose for our lives..

LIFE'S JOURNEY

As we go about life's journeys finding time to celebrate is inevitable to be able to praise the lord with music song and dance is an expression of art that should inspire us to celebrate the coming of the lord. The presence of the lord, and the spirit of the lord Holy in my walk. Someone plan a walk for a worthy cause they ask for money to sponsor them they take the walk but so too in our daily journey with God we work so that others may get the benefit by our intercession by prayer by holy example. But not everyone could take this walk. The invitation is limited to a select few only those with pure motives and guiltless actions can have access to God would you be able to take this walk if not ask God to examine today my motives and actions. God thank you for Jesus power to cleanse and to lift me. I need your guidance to help others to believe that they do can walk to and stand in holy places with you let it be by my walk others will come to Front Line Ministries. What must I do to be saved? Also I met a security guard and talked about marriage and my journey here to Seattle and God is transforming me into his image Praise God. God has selected me as his treasured possession. We are forever worth more to God than anything we can imagine. We are sealed as his priceless inheritance he made us in his image and called me to be Extraordinary. We are gifts to God from God. God has hidden us in his heart where his treasure reside. Love for God demonstrated in obedience, our joy in the Lord that honor's him with thanksgiving and peace in the Lord that produces patience. And without faith we give up on God's purpose for our lives..

TOO MUCH OF ME

JUDGES 7; 1-8

Many times the working, methods, and ways of God seem to make absolutely no sense. There seems to be no rhyme or reason to why God does things the way he does. We see it in his choosing of Israel to be his people and the nation through whom the Messiah would come He said that it wasn't because of their great strength or numbers that he chose Israel, but because of their smallness and weakness. Because of his love and covenant Deuteronomy 4;37 and because he loved thy fathers, therefore he chose their seed after them, and brought thee out in his sight with his mighty power out of Egypt. He chose David with a sling and one stone to save his people from Goliath- 1Samuel 17:40 and he took his staff in his hand, and chose him five smooth stones out of the brook, and put them in a shepherd's bag which he had, even in a scrip and sling was in his hand: and drew near the Philistine. The Apostle Paul was least of the Apostles and saints, yet the chief fest of sinners 1 Corinthians 6:4 If then ye have judgments of things pertaining to this life, set them to judge who are the least esteemed in the church. Ephesians 3:8 unto me, who am less than the least of the saints, is this grace given, that I should preach among the Gentiles the unsearchable riches of Christ. Gideon was the weakest of the weak and the poorest of the poor-Judges6:15. And he said unto him, oh my Lord, where with shall I save Israel? Behold my family is poor in Manasseh, and I am the least in my father's house. Often God waits until we are down to "Gideon's 300" to answer our praycrs- do mighty work.

Gideon's Position (vs1)

1. Pitched by the well of Harod. They were in great fear because they were far outnumbered by the Midianites 32,000 to a host".
2. **In Hebrew Harod means fountain of trembling, affliction.**

3. Are you pitched at the fountain of trembling and affliction today? Are your resources depleted? Bank account exhausted.

4. That's the kind of place that God works best —Isaiah 59:19 when the enemy shall come in like a flood the Spirit of the Lord shall lift up a standard against him.

5. The host of Midianites was camped by the hill of Moreh. In Hebrew Moreh means early rain! Elijah's cloud the size of a man's fist in 1 Kings 18:41-45.

6. God was about to bring Victory- the early rain was going to fall again! God was going to destroy the Midianites and once again poor out a rain that would eventually turn into a harvest.

7. Today we have the latter rain- Power of the Holy Spirit!

Gideon's Position (vs2)

1. The people are too many. Gideon needed to find God as his source of power and strength. 32,000 were too many.

2. It wasn't that Gideon couldn't defeat the Midianites with that number. Clearly he could have.

3. Gideon, not God would have receive the Glory(vs2)

4. The life of Faith is not for weak of Heart(vs3)

5. 22,000 were still too many. 10,000 were still too many.

6. God then did the incredible and tested Gideon's faith (vs4-7). One of the hardest lessons God's people seem to have a hard time learning is never do in the flesh what God must do in the Spirit. Had Gideon used 32, 000, 22, 000, 10,000 it would have been a victory by the flesh.

7. The people are too many. Are you down to your 300 yet? God will meet whatever your need is by his power!

Gideon's Promise from God (vs7, 8)

1. God gave a wonderful two part promise to Gideon:
   - "l will save you".
   - "l will deliver the Midianites into your hands."

   I believe that there is someone here today that God will not only save from your situation but deliver the enemy into to your hands- will let you take what the "Midianites" did to do harm, and give you a blessing from it.

   Before you hear the sound of faith you must be in a posture of readiness only 300 of the men were in a posture of readiness where they could respond quickly.

There are four tests we face:

- Fear Test
- Faith Test
- The Focus Test
- Fruitfulness Test

Do you pass?

- I can
- I will
- I must

By the three hundred men that lapped will I save you? They were evidently the most alert of the group, snatching up the water in the cupped hands and lapping it like a dog. This is a parallel and parable for all of life. Spiritual nourishment is to be obtained as one move along the common paths of daily experience. Those who wait for some special occasion, Sometime of retreat and meditation, some dream or prophet ecstasy to mark the coming of God's spirit, are apt to continue waiting. Beside our simplest paths there are the running brooks of Spiritual refreshment, and we may stoop and drink as we move from task to task. Railway engines take on water from track-level troughs and with great roar and splashing gather up their " nourishment" without missing an instant in their schedule A.C. Mcgiffert, when president of Union Theological Seminary, startled a group of students by saying that he had practically abandoned any stated times of prayer. Then he when on to reassure them by adding that he found it possible to place all the experience of each day in the setting of prayer, so that all along the way he was being refreshed and renewed. For most people that achievement is far off, but who can doubt that it should be our goal? The basic spiritual lesson it teaches is that a few with God can overcome a great host without him. We are becoming more and more conscious of the importance of small minority groups.

Get Out of our own way

Face it before God can fix it

Tea Bag in a Hot Water World

GOING DEEPER

EZEKIEL 47:1-47:12

How much of God are you experiencing?

Within this scripture I see that we can be at four basic levels in our walk with God... Four varying depths of relationship with God. These differing depths are choice, not God's we decide how far we are willing to go w/ Jesus.

1. **Ankle Deep-ankle bitters:** you step in... Illustration: Worlds of fun the cement was

so hot in the scorching sun that we literally had to run on our tippy toes to keep our feet from burning. We would take short breaks in the shaded areas or puddle. It was only temporary relief until we got into the water. You step in.. You visit God once or twice a week to say hello. You like listen to worship but you never enter in. You like the "cooling" feeling to be here, but you don't allow yourself to become a part. You think the people here are nice all and all, But you never build any relationships. You don't feel like getting wet, maybe you don't even want to be here- excuses are a dime a dozen You don't want change you think that you're just fine on the shore. Your feet might not be burning anymore, but the rest of you still getting burned. Temporary relief doesn't bring eternal results. God doesn't just want to be your aspirin ...He wants you to go deeper with him so that you can experience hi fullness! You can't do that standing on the shore ankle deep.

2. **Knee Deep-knee knockers:** here is where you roll up your pants and go in a bit deeper you actually start to sing during worship instead of talking or looking around you get into the game time and have fun.. but

   A. You're still not willing to go all the way with Jesus...you're holding back

    B. Your afraid of what people may think or say your knees are knocking

    C. You become a fence rider —Hypocrite you're still too close to shore. You come to church you're in the water a litter, having a good time but tomorrow you'll be on the shore again in the world.

3. **Waist Deep-wasters:** This is where it really starts to get somewhat uncomfortable...the water starts hitting some very sensitive areas; we're not sure if we really like it or not.

    A. We've come to cross road where commitment insects with passion.

    B. There is no halfway with God no middle ground (Rev: 3:16) People that only go halfway look like idiots. Only going halfway leads to backsliding.

4. Swimmers move past how they feel and worship anyway.

Swimmer move past how they look to others and take a stand for righteousness.

Swimmers move past what they want and fulfill god's commands to reach everyone, everywhere with the message of Christ.

Swimmers are survivors they're not just treading water to stay afloat. They're swimming.

In pursuit of God to save the world.

Swimmers experience the fullness of God!

Why be a swimmer?

1. The water of God is Fresh- when we are moving across the pool.
2. Everything in the water is alive- no floaters
3. The water will help us to prosper!-Fruit that won't fail, leaves that won't wither (Ps.l:l3;Jer. 17:7-8)
4. We will bring food and healing to the world! Food — I am the bread of life, he who comes to me never go hungry, he who believe in me never be thirsty. "(Jn.6:35) healing-supernatural recovery both physical and spiritual. Holy Spirit it is a picture of a Christian yielded to the Holy Spirit. Are you at Ankle depth, Knee depth, Waist depth or are you swimming in the river of God?
5. **Ankles** —Achilles—tendon our Achilles tendon is located at our ankles if our Achilles tendon is damaged we cannot walk for 6 months similarly we become very vulnerable to the Devil's attacks when our foundation is weak.
6. **Knee Depth** —Knees are joints that cause us to run. If you damage your knees, you will have very little movement of your legs. You can barely move your legs. God wants

us to surrender the running of our life to him. He wants us to run on the "Knees of Prayer". When we are on our knees it's a sign of our surrender to God. Our faith must be strengthen by prayer

7. **Waist depth** —At the waist level in a flowing river we are beginning to lose control of our movement in the water. We cannot run anymore at waist level. God wants us to let go of our strength and control of our lives to him. The waist (loins) is the area where all reproductive organs are located. When we surrender our lives to God he will bring fruitfulness to our lives. Fruitfulness will come together with truth and righteousness in our lives.

8. **Swimming depth**- at swimming depth our feet cannot touch the ground we have very little control of our body, at fast currents in the river the current carry us along the river. God wants full control and navigation rights of our life. The river is deepest and the current is fastest at the centre. We need to be in the centre of God's will before we can experience the fullness of the river of God. At the swimming depth the river takes us wherever the river flows the river control us we do not control the Holy Spirit.

ELDER TREMELLJ. COLLINS
(A TEA BAG IN A HOT WATER WORLD BOOK)

MASTER THE 4 PHASES OF A BREAKTHROUGH

ICHRONICLES **14:8-14:17**

"TEA BAG IN A HOT WATER WORLD"
Main Idea:

- Breaking through the status quo barrier is a cyclical process not a onetime event.
- This process consists of 4 distinct but necessary phases God takes us through on the road to the next level in our spiritual lives.

I want you to see if you can notice a pattern floating to the surface of the text.

The pattern of a Breakthrough

There is a pattern that emerges here it's a 4 identifiable phases. I call this the pattern of a Breakthrough. I want to walk you through these 4 phases.

Phase#1: I GO THROUGH A CRISIS.

This is the first phase on the road to reaching the next level in your life. God allows crisis to come into your life that pushes up against your belief in God. Something takes place in your life that puts your back against a wall. It's called a crisis. How many of you have ever experienced a crisis? I want you to notice David's crisis in verses 8-9. Now the philistines heard that David had been anointed king over all Israel, all Philistines went up to search for David. And David heard of it and went out against them."V.9" Then the Philistines went out and made a raid on the valley of Rephaim." David was anointed king over Israel. He's promoted and all things going well when all of a sudden a crisis comes into his life. David's crisis had a name. It' called the Philistines. The Philistines are mentioned 286times in the Old Testament and their land is mentioned 8 times. What I'm sayings is that God gives the Philistines a lot of air time in the Old Testament. They're mentioned a lot. And when they are mention it is usually because they are opposing something God wants to do. Here we see them opposing God's Leader David. David's crisis was a military crisis. Just like a gigantic chess match the Philistines in verse8 came up to search for David to kill him. David countered with his own move in verse 9-8 by coming out against the Philistines army. The Philistines in a strategic and defiant move raided a valley in Jewish territory valley it turns out that was a direct route to the capital city of Jerusalem David's stronghold. David was stunned. David was scared. David was smack dab in the middle of a crisis. Experiencing a crisis that's the first phase in experiencing a breakthrough in your life. God allows you to face a challenge or daunting obstacle that pushes up against **your Belief and Faith** in God. Everybody faces different kinds of crisis. I made a list that people sometimes face and I want to read them to you and see if you've faced any of these in your life.

Common Crisis People often face

1. The loss of a valued relationship such as breaking up with a boyfriend or girlfriend, or divorce. The dissolving of a long time partnership.
2. Failing a class in school or falling an entire grade.
3. Losing one's Job.
4. Bankruptcy
5. Declining health of you or someone you care about, Health issues usually send us into crisis mode.
6. The death of someone close to you these are just a few but they are some of the more intense kind of crisis we can face.

Question!

Why God does allow us to go through a crisis in order to break through to the next level?

The reason is because life on the average daily tone is not enough to break us out of our status quo routines, our status quo ruts or our status quo mind-set. So God allows us to feel the heat. The Crisis takes you off Auto-Pilot. It wake you up and Slaps our spiritual senses back to reality. Sometimes we ask for these things by decisions we make and sometimes we don't ask for them. I like how one author describes this kind of experience. He says:" They are voluntary and involuntary. These proving moments comes to us ready or not. Sometimes we make decisions that invite them: and other times we are surprised by them. It is the difference between starving and fasting. One is voluntary and the other is Involuntary." David's crisis was involuntary He'd done nothing to bring this on himself. It came into his life and David didn't ask for it. He didn't want it, but one thing is for sure, he had to respond to it. The most difficult crisis I've ever experience came in 1992 and 2009 when I went through two divorces they were crisis tea bags in hot water. Back to David and allow me to share with you the next phase of the breakthrough pattern.

Phase#2 1 go to God

First I GO THROUGH A CRISIS.

THEN I GO TO GOD. Notice verse 10with me: and David inquired of God saying "shall I go up against the Philistines? Will you deliver them into my hand? The Lord said "GO up, for I will deliver them into your hand." The way that you and I respond when we're in crisis is important to God. Our Reponses often determines whether we go up or whether we give up. How we response determines whether we'll be able to break the status quo in our life. **Dr. John Maxwell says; "These experiences are like Tea Bags in Hot Water: They bring out the true colors inside." A crisis simply reveals what is on the inside of you. The crisis that David went through revealed a dependence on God.** This crisis motivated David to call on God for divine assistance now not everyone responds this way to a crisis some people get angry at others or at God when crisis comes to their lives. But not David, at least not on this occasion this time he simply prayed. I can tell you when I went through two marriages I had to pray and asked God for help. What else could I do? I was in a crisis and I had nowhere else to turn. So I cried out to God in my heart and begged for help. Have you ever been there? Have you ever been at that point in your life? I've been there David was there now, let me share with you phase 3. After you go through a crisis and go to God... **Phase#3: I GO ON FAITH.GOD** answered

David in verse10 and said to him: "GO UP, for I will deliver them into your hand." God answers David's prayer. God speaks into David's life loud and clear. There no question that it is God who spoke and there's no question about what God promised. God promised David victory. Now at this point David has a choice. Will I believe what God said, or will I go with my gut? Will David go on Faith or go on Feelings? **Dr. HENRY BLACKBERRY, co-author of the book Experiencing God, describes David's crisis this way; "David was a faithful servant of the Lord's. David refused to rely on human wisdom for guidance. He asked for God's direction. Was this crisis of belief since God said he would give David victory over the Philistines? Yes! David still had to decide what he believed about God. He had to trust God to do what he said he would do." What did David do? How did he respond to God? Look at verse10. It says "The Lord said to him, go up, for I will deliver them into to your hand". And notice what David did in verse II; so they went up to Baal Perazim, and David defeated them there..."Go said 'IGO UP". David said "I will" David obeyed the Lord and did exactly what God told him to do. David was going on Faith. Going through a divorce in 2009 1 was going through a crisis I was going to God. And now, like David before me, I needed to go on faith, trusting God to do what he knew would be best. Right then and there I made a decision. My prayer went something like this; "God this servant I am going through a divorce and I give her to you.**

I take my heart and give it to you. And ask you to please spare the pain I feel I trust you Lord;" Some things in life you can't talk your way out of. Something's in life you can't work your way out of. Something's in life you can't buy your way out of. Something's in life you can only trust your way out of. Some of you are going through a crisis today and you have to make a decision. In fact the word crisis comes from a greek word that means decision. That same greek word sometimes translated judgment. A crisis is a turning point, a moment of truth in our lives when make a concrete decision to follow God and trust him or not to trust God and walk away from him. Now let's share the **# 4; I GO UP**.IN THE BREAKTHROUGH PROCESS.I go up to the next level I breakthrough into a **new realm; higher dimension of living**. I break the status quo barrier I graduate from one grade to another. After **David went through the first 3 phases of the process and had to come and decide he was going to go on faith**, look what happened to David in verse 11; **"Then David said God has broken through my enemies by my hand a breakthrough of water"**. David experienced his much needed breakthrough. Just like I said what I went through coming to Seattle, Was after getting married and being HOMELESS FOR AWILE. Just like David I had gone through all 4 phases. Not one phase was skipped. Look with me at verse 13; "Then the philistines once again made a raid on the valley." Wait a minute I thought David had just defeated them? He had. But they reared their ugly head again. Problems often do that. **Have you ever faced the same problem more than once? Do you know anybody that has ever gotten more than one speeding ticket? Do you know anybody that has more than one dui? I do.** Sometimes we face the same crisis more than once, **the first time David faces this crisis, and he was inexperienced. The second time he was a veteran. He knew what to do. Verse 14 tells us; 'Therefore David inquired of God...? It's a pattern you'll see repeated all throughout your life as a Christian. It's just the way God works. I go through a crisis, I Go to God; I go on Faith, I Go Up. I go through a crisis, I Go to God; I go on Faith, I Go UP. Rawhide!!! So I'm sitting here and thinking to myself I've been here before. I know what to do I've got to go to God." I fully expect that in a few weeks or months I'm going through another crisis and I'll have to go through all 4 phases again so that I can continue to graduate to a higher level of living with God. What are you going through today? Have you made a decision to trust God with it?**

ELDER TREMELL J. COLLINS
"A TEA BAG IN A HOT WATER WORLD

TOSSIN-N TURNIN
JOB 7:4

(KING JAMES VERSION)

"When I lie down, I say When shall I arise, and the night be gone? And I am full of tossing to and from unto the dawning of the day"

(New King James Version)

"When I lie down, I say When I arise, and the night be ended? For I have had my fill of tossing till dawn"

(Contemporary English Version)

"I pray for night to end, but it stretches out while I toss and turn."

In July of 1961 a singer by the name of Bobby Lewis recorded a song titled "Tossing-n-Turning". For twenty-three weeks the song road the charts eventually hitting the number 1 spot in both the pop and rhythm & blues categories. The words and melody of the song, which was the only monster hit recorded by Bobby Lewis, was on the lips and in the minds of practically every teenager of that time who ever had been in love. In the song **Bobby Lewis sang to a woman who had evidently done some "love thing" to him that cause him not to be able to sleep at night. He said, I couldn't sleep at all last night, just thinking of you." He said "things weren't right-cause; I was tossing and turning, tossing and turning, tossing and turning all night." And then he went on to describe everything he went through that restless evening. He said, "l kicked the blankets on the floor, turn my pillow upside-down. I never, never did before. But I was tossing' and turn in, tossing and turning all night. He said I jumped out of bed turned on the light pulled the shade went to the kitchen for a bite... Rolled up the shade turned off the light I jumped back in bed it was the middle of the night! The clock down stairs was striking**

four couldn't get you off my mind. I heard the milk man at the door because I was tossing and turning all night!" I can't say that I've ever been in love like that (except maybe the night before I was about to get married) but in my life, I have spent many nights "tossing and turning over problems! How many of you today that the trouble of life can cause you to lose sleep? Sometimes your troubles can be so great you pray for morning to hurry up and come, so at least you can go to work and try to forget about your troubles for a little while. Trouble will test you and find out what you're made of everyone here had a situation or problem that seemed to have no solution nor rhyme nor reason why it was happening to you. Especially if you're a Christian! Sometimes it seems like when you are trying to live for God that troubles comes from everywhere! Sometimes the troubles of this Christian Life seem so UN fair! But you must understand that many are the afflictions of the righteous. "In other words, righteous folks have to go through!. That word righteous is the key word there First of all, understand that there are two types of righteousness: One is to be "self righteous" that means we think we are better than everyone else! A person who thinks they are righteous because they don't cuss, drink, smoke, or do drugs and so on but looks down on those who do without offering a word of Godly advice is self —righteous. But listen just because you don't do any of those things does not make you righteous because folks in church don't do any of that but they 're guilty of other stuff like not speaking to their neighbor like holding a grudge against somebody like wanting to be scene or recognized for what they do in the church! To be righteous of God is to be made a new again! Paul said in **2 Corinthians 5:17** "Therefore if any man be in Christ, he is a new creature: old things are passed away: behold al things are become new." IN the text we find a man who is undergoing a severe testing of our faith only Job here is unaware that he is the subject of spiritual contest between God and Satan.

The book of Job is called one of the most profound books in the entire bible for it confronts head on the toughest question of Christian existence, "Why do the righteous suffer and the evil prosper? Or as every Christian person has cried out over the ages, what did I do to deserve this? Why is this happening to me? "Have you ever asked God questions like while you're in a midnight situation that caused you to lose sleep?

Lord I thought I was your boy...

Lord I thought I was your girl...

You told me that you'd make my enemies be my foot stools...

You told me that I would eat the fat, drink the sweet and be merry...

But here I am "Tossing- n-turning- tossing-n-turning all night!

You know the story if you've studied your bible Job suffered a tremendous series of calamities that wiped out all the he value. In one tragic day Job lost all his possessions, and his seven children. Subsequently, lost his health, and was afflicted with a terrible disease that left him covered with boils from head to foot. To top it all off, his wife turned against him and suggested that he curse God and commit suicide. But look at Job and learn... Despite all of these pressures, Job trust in the mercy and love and grace of God and refuses to do what Satan is trying to get him to do—that is curse God and die! What we must understand is that in every trial of this Christian there are two purposes in operation: Satan has his purpose, and God has his. Satan's purpose here was to use the pain of Job's illness to afflict his body. Next to use the well- intentioned comfort of his friends to irritate his soul (because his so-called three friends- Bildad, Eliphaz and Zophar-were trying to tell him that he must have done something wrong and as a result, God was punishing him) and thirdly, to use the silence of God to assault his spirit and break his faith. But God' purpose here is to teach Job some truths that he never knew before (1) to deepen his theology. (2) To help him understand God much better and (3) to provide a demonstration for all sufferers in all ages, to bring them assurance that God knows what he's doing! When you are going through, you have got to believe that God is still in control and he knows what he's doing! And when you recognize that God is in control you can sleep at night when storms of life are raging!

When you recognize that God is in control... You can smile when your money is funny and your change is strange! When you recognize that God is in control... You can hold your head up when situations have almost gotten the best of you! When you recognize that God is in control... When you lay in bed at night and can't count your sheep, you can count your blessings! Count them and see what the Lord has done! Matter of fact you ought to make a blessing list count all the times when your back was up against the wall and God has brought you out! I guarantee you won't be able to write it down in one day, though, for the song writer said **"If I had to tell it I could not tell it all!"** well if that's so easy then why didn't Job do it? Understand again that Job didn't know of the contest between Satan and God. He didn't know Satan showed up in heaven and petitioned God for a chance to beat him down. The only reason we know is because we have the evidence of scripture. Job didn't have that that's why he speaks as he does in verse4 of chapter7: He says " I'm going though so much now that when I lie down, I say when I shall arise and the night be gone? Because I am tired of tossing to and from unto the dawning of day." I'm talking about: tossing-n — Turin". But you see you have it better than Job had it. We have the assurance of God's Holy Word! Yes that's why God gave us his word in complete form, because God knows that if Satan tried to do it to Job (a man who was perfect) he'll try to do it to you and me (who are far less than perfect). And next time you find yourself "Tossing-n Turin just speaks to your spirit and say this isn't anything but a test, I'm going to wait on God to bring me out! How many of you know God will bring you out? **You see your test today is directed and connected to three things:**

- It's connected to your past

- It's connected to your present

- It's connected to your future

Your past connections is that God saw something in you that needed to change for the better, and so he brought me out of my dark past and place me in the present light! But now God didn't say that my life would be a flowery bed of eaves. But we must understand that your futures blessings are connected to how we handle are present sufferings. In other words, If God sees that you can handle what you're going through right now; he'll bless you on tomorrow with a blessing you won't have room to receive! In other words if you can endure tonight's.

Tossing and Turin... Tomorrow God has promised that your:

- Problem will turn into your praise...

- Your trails will turn into your triumphs...

- Your worry will turn into joy...

- Your test will turn into your testimony...

- You'll no longer be a victim you'll be a victor!

No wonder David was able to say, **"Weeping endure for a night, but joy comes in the morning!"** I stopped by on my way to heaven to give somebody a good word: "It's almost morning time!" Rise, shine and give God the Glory! Thank you Job for letting us looks behind the curtain of God's purposes and see the blessings that hang on the outcome of our struggles. And so today I want to tell someone what you said," all of my appointed time I will wait until my change comes!" Thank you Job for going through! You've been an encouragement to those of us who must go through times of suffering. It's not always because we are sinful. Sometimes it is and we know it when it is. But Job, We know form scripture that he didn't deserve it.

- I might have to spend a few sleepless nights but I'll wait!

- I may be lied on but I'll wait!

- I may be broke today but I'll wait!

- I may be talked about and made fun of but I'll wait!

- I may be criticized, but I'll wait!

- My marriage may be on the rocks today but I'll wait!

- I'll wait until my change comes!

Listen the climax of Job's situation is not restoration of his property or the provision of a new family. No the climax is when God reveals himself and hence Job (in chapter 42) says **"Surely I spoken of things I did not understand, things too wonderful for me to know. My ears had heard of you but now my eyes have seen you"** Job learned Go's character through suffering. God revealed his power and might and wisdom. And in doing so he also revealed his mercy and compassion. Sometimes suffering is not always punishment. Sometimes it's to give us a more real experience of God of who he is and what he's like. God wants our suffering to lead us to endurance and stronger faith and trust in him. Understand that many are the afflictions of the righteous"(or the anointed) then if you are going through today you must be worth something tell somebody today that you are worth something to God!"

If Job waited on the Lord, Why can't I? Tell somebody to wait a little longer?

God sees you're tossing and turning. "I see the Son about to come up" Not the S-u-n, but Son. I see the Son of God about to show up in somebody's situation and honey when he shows up he's going to show out!.

GOD USES A SURGE
OF PROBLEMS

If the book of Acts had a sound track, at the beginning of chapter 27, the music would start off slowly and ominously. Or Maybe that music from jaws. You know (Da Dum, Da Dum...) and then in the back ground you'd hear the wind blowing and the waves rising. And then maybe that music from the Wizard of Oz. you know, when the wicked witch is on her way to get Dorothy. And the hurricane hits in full force. And the waves crash against the hull. The crew is screaming, the captain is shouting orders. The tension mounts all hope is gone and then the climax music. Here comes the hero. I've been accused of having an overactive imagination, but for me it helps this book come alive! This is not just some dry history book; this is a human drama at its most dramatic. Storms and shipwreck and lives hanging in the balance. But you know the main reason I like this chapter? Because it's not just about how God dealt with a bunch of guys on a ship 2,000 years ago. This is how God deals with us right now, today!

Chippie the parakeet never saw it coming. One second he was peacefully perched in his cage. The next he was sucked in, washed up, and blown over. The problems began when Chippie's owner decided to clean Chippies cage with a vacuum cleaner. She removed the attachments from the end of the hose and stuck it in the cage. The phone rang, and she turned to pick it up. She'd barely said "hello" when "ssssopp!" Chippie got sucked in. The bird owner grasp, but put down the phone, turn off the vacuum, and open the bag. There was Chippie still alive, but stunned. Since the bird was covered with dust and soot, she grabbed him and raced to the bathroom, turned on the faucet, and held Chippie under the running water. Then realizing the Chippie was soaked and shivering, she did what any compassionate bird owner would do she reached for the hair dryer and blasted the pet with hot air. Poor Chippie never knew what hit him. A few days after the trauma, the reporter who'd initially written about the event contacted Chippie's owner to see how the bird was recovering. "Well," she replied, Chippie doesn't sing much anymore he just sits and stares." Ever felt that way? Sucked in, washed up and blown over? Sure you have? Like these men we'll read about, you've been thrown around. You've been plunged into the eye of the storm, and if that hasn't happened yet, yet just wait its coming. Maybe it's family disaster. Death or disease or divorce. Maybe it's a financial or you just lost a job or gotten heavy in debt. Maybe your tempest has come in the form of depression, whose gale force winds can rip down your sails and leave you dead in the water, feeling overwhelmed and underpowered. I don't know what it is or what it will be in your life, but I know these storms will come! And the lesson of Acts 27 for you and me is that God delivers us from the storm of life... We begin on calm waters in Acts 27 and verse 1. God uses a surge of problems sometimes to direct us, to inspect us, to correct us, to connect us, to protect us, to perfect us, to project us. God Direct Us- sometimes God must light a fire under you to get us moving. Problems often point us in in a new direction and motivate us to change? Is God trying to get our attention? To Correct Us -some lessons we learn only through pain and failure it likely that as a child your parents told you not to touch a hot stove. Sometimes we only learn the value of something by losing it. Inspects Us- People are like tea bags if you want to know what's inside them just drop them in hot water. Has God ever tested your faith with a problem what do problems reveal about you? To Connect Us — When someone dies in a family loved one gather from far and near for the funeral people want to be together when in trouble. To Protect Us —A problem can be a blessing in disguise if it prevents you from being harmed by something more serious. T Prefect Us- Problem when responded to correctly are character builders. God's more interested in your character than your comfort your relationship to God and your character are the only two things you're going to take with you into eternity. To Project Us — the surge of the trouble focuses us outwardly on what is most important it furthers God's cause it is not the burdens of life that weigh us down it is how we handle them? Trouble is simply the factory God's using to manufacture the right type of product in our lives. The blueness of a wound clean Seth away evil (Proverb 20:30). Trials and testing come very near to the finish line whenever there is a gigantic open door there always adversaries right before the door. That's where they hang out temptation of quitting before you reach the end comes from looking at how far you are from the finish line we spend our time thinking about what shall we need to finish rather than maximizing the strength that we already have. Make a choice finish strong with what you have. 7 ways God will use a surge problem in our lives.

Direct Us-Proverbs 20:30

To Correct Us- Psalms 119: 71

To Inspect Us- James 1:2-3

To Connect Us-psalms 119:67

To Protect Us- Genesis 50:20

To Perfect Us- Romans 5:3-4, Psalms 71:19-21, Romans 8:28

TO Project Us- Phil.1:12, Isa.40:31, James 1:12

Turn the lens of your Life so you can catch more of the light that is always available for healing!

You can't change yesterday but you can change today. And To live many days as possible as if I were on vacation an adventure...

Christ is no security against storms but he's perfect in storms he does guarantee a safe landing.

Two looks at life how they help or hinder Looking back beholding pain Looking ahead is making progress!

STORMS WILL COME

Jesus will be with us in the storms

Jesus will calm the storms

It's only in the storms that we really know who Jesus the perfect storm......

Life is a busy enterprise. It seems there are always more things to do places to go, and people to meet. And while none of us would want a life without meaningful things to do, the fast pace threatens to rob us of the quietness that we need. When we've driving a car, stop signs and other warning us to slow down are reminders that to be safe can't have our foot on the accelerator all the time. We need those kinds of reminders in all aspects of our lives. - Joe Stowell.....

A HEART SHIFT TWO

Waking up miles away from where you want to be. Far too many marriages increasingly more and more all across the country who wake up one day to discover their marriage that's in ruins confusing is that there was never a clear —cut wreaking —ball reason for the collapse. In the marriage there was no adultery, no drugs or alcohol addiction issues no job loss that caused incredible financial pressures no piling on by intrusive in laws that finally because so heavy it shattered the relationship despite all this, the relationship was in ruins and seemingly over such small things. Tremell and others represent people in crisis but have you ever felt like? In your health, at home or even in your heart for God. Have you ever felt that the place you're at is close to where you ever thought you be? If so you're not alone and you're picked up the right book, Paul 's words " Let Him Who thinks he stands take heed that he does not fall" (1 CorlO;12) I have found that it is incredibly easy for all but a few in one or more important areas of our lives. In fact it's not just individuals w ho wakes up one day Far from where they want to be. In the scripture an entire home church got wakeup calls that despite all their good works things were terribly wrong. (Putting things on auto pilot) just assume we'll end up where we want to go. It's time we make a heart shift. How about a 2 degree change can ruin or renew your life. You'll miss not only your point of orbital entry, but you'll miss the moon by measly 11,121 miles. Just 2 degrees off from where you blast off. Just be 2 degrees off from a right heart attitude add, in enough time, and distance and an entire church can end up miles from God's Heart. In my counseling practice that same explanation fit like a frame around many troubled marriages I'd seen. Be just a few degrees off as a couple and don't bother to make any genuine course correction over the months and years and then watch how you woke up one day and discover you're emotionally miles apart. After all what's easier to do? Make 180 degree change back towards his wife or just turn 2 degrees towards a stranger I formed a tangible picture in my mind and provided an answers to much of the emotional spiritual and even physical wreckage I'd seen for decades What's more, it open my eyes to passage after passage in scripture that talk about the importance of small things in Life of faith, peace, and rest. The Idea is that a small 2 degrees could change their life for worse given the gradual workings of time. Amazingly even small shifts in a positive direction could move a person from ruin to renewal. A gap between couples in conflict? That bridge is what I call a Heart Shift, and the way we cross it is through 2 degree changes. C.S. Lewis uses the word charity to describe just such a secret path. About good and evil in Mere Christianity Lewis talks about a word called charity for Lewis this word has a two part definition. One part has to do with forgiveness but the primary definition of what it means to "DO well" as a Christian. Is by extending charity to others a word very different from what we normally refer to as charity? Good and evil both increase at compound interest. That's why the little decisions you and I make every day are of such infinite importance. If making a heart shift requires facing our pride it also demands that we be honest about the degree of anger we carry in our lives. Anger turned inward or towards others pushes us into darkness and blinds us to something as small as a 2 degree change. And linked with anger is unwillingness to forgiveness hand in hand with holding on to anger is an unwillingness to forgive. In biblical Greek the word LUO, translated '(Forgiveness" in English literally means "To Untie the Knot". Most people equate the word change with a one hundred- eighty- degree turn a feat so overwhelming they don't know where to begin. Yet a 2 degree change in our spiritual life's our home life, and even our health can lead us closer to God's heart and the ones we love. You can let the 2 degree difference move you in a positive, freeing, and fulfilling direction. The key to making lasting changes in our lives lies in making a series of 2 degree changes. If you're driving a brand new, finely tuned automobile and it starts to veer off the road, you don't jerk the steering wheel 180 degrees. You may not even be aware of it, but you're making a series of positive, 2 Degree changes to keep the car going straight down the road... It is said that it's about 217,614 miles from earth to the moon but depending on the moon's orbit around the earth if off 2 degrees from blast off you'll miss the moon by 11,121 miles. Add in enough time and distance and be just 2 degrees off you'll miss the target by miles..

HEAR SHIFT BY JOHN TRENT

NOTE BY ELDER TREMELL J. COLLINS

A STORM IN A TEACUP

MATT 14; 21-14:33

Britannica .com says, a storm is "a generic term, popularly used to describe a large variety of atmospheric disturbances, ranging from ordinary rain showers and snowstorms to thunderstorms, wind and wind-related disturbances such as gales, tornadoes, tropical cyclones, and sandstorms (brittannica.com). Storms are dangerous, destructive and deadly, and they easily obliterate people, damage property and overrun protection in their path.

Storms are mostly powerful winds in the air. The winds have knocked down the trees in our courtyard forced out a panel of glass and blown down the storage door. Trying to open one's car door without hitting a neighbor's car is a challenge! The strongest winds in 2006, while nothing compared to Chicago record 88mph winds, clocked in at 58mph. just after Jesus had fed the 5,000 men , not including women and children ,he sent the disciples on a boat to the other side, while he dismissed the crowd, he went up a mountain and spent the night in prayer. Mean while the boat, far from shore was buffeted out to sea by the winds and the waves. Jesus went out to the disciples, but the terrified disciples thought they saw a ghost. When peter realized it was Jesus, he asked for a miracle: to walk on water. He succeeded momentarily, but fear, panic and doubts seized him, and he sank like a rock. Why do fears attack, weaken and immobilize our hearts, resolve and faith? Is fear a trap or a test? And how does Jesus presence remove the peril of fear? Check your facts Immediately Jesus made the disciples get into the boat and goon ahead of him to the other side, while he dismissed the crowd. He when up on a mountainside by himself to pray. When evening came, He was there alone, but the boat was already a considerable distance from land, buffeted by the waves because the wind was against it During the fourth watch of the night Jesus went out to them walking on the lake.(Matt14:21-25). In this passage, the Greek word "phobia" for fear or afraid" looms large, draws close and appears menacingly in verse 26-27 and 30. Some said the acronym for fear stands for **"<u>false evidence appearing real.</u>"** My favorite is **"<u>Forget Everything And Run!</u>"** As Franklin Roosevelt once said, "The only thing we have to fear is fear itself." It is hard to explain why people fear more than just dogs, snakes or insects. Time magazine reported that people suffer from at least 500 human fears- from Acrophobia (the fear of heights), Claustrophobia (fear of enclosed spaces). The fear of colors, animals, and people objects. And Agoraphobia (crushing, paralyzing terror of anything outside the safety of the home. (Times 4/02/01 "What Scares Us"). Jesus first responded to the disciples fears before addressing Peter's fears. He finally knew what terrorized the disciples but yet chose to test them again After all the master made the decision to send them to the other side directly into the eye of the storm. Instead of hurrying to join the disciples, Jesus took time to pray further, Jesus knew the disciples had problems though they were a considerable distance away. The parallel Passage of Mark 6:48 records that in his praying Jesus saw "the disciples straining at the oars, with the wind in their path and the waves hammering them like a nail, throwing them like packages and blowing them like chaff, before he later took action in the fourth watch of the night. Jesus knew of their rough passage, their difficult plight and their terrible predicament. The omniscient and prescient Savior was right in not taking immediate action. Although it made for a long night to the disciples, it was not a losing fight. The parallel account in John 6:17 Says it was a dark night, not a doomed night. The waves put up a good fight but the disciples put up a better fight. They were resourceful, remarkable and resilient. The boat was tossed but not torpedoed by the waves. In fact the disciples did such a good job that Jesus continued with the priority of praying. Contrary to reader's traditional understanding, the fishermen were not overwhelmed, overmatched or overpowered at this point. They were overworked, overawed, overextended but they were not over their heads. The fishermen had more experience with the deep, more tricks up their sleeves and more knowledge of the sea than most people. At no time was the sea winning and the disciples losing; they were locked in a fierce struggle. At worst, the disciples were behind, but not beat; down but not out. The boat was surviving well not sinking fast. Many readers confuse this passage with another boating incident- the first lake crossing where the disciples boat was covered" in water (Mark4; 37, Matt 8:24).This time they were "buffeted" or "tossed" by the plummeted but not perishing. The fishermen navigated the troubled waters and rough seas proficiently, professionally and perfectly. The disciple hung on, rowed hard and brought time. Further, they had learned from their experience and were not crying for divine help. According to John 6; 19) Jesus did not get to the disciples until they were "three or three and a half miles from shore." Matthew 14:25 states that Jesus left dry land for the wet waters in the fourth watch" or last quarter of the night. The first watch or the first quarter is 6-9p.m. and the last is 3-6a.m. so the crew was doing well for many hours as Jesus left them to fight the storms by themselves. When the disciples saw him walking on the lake, they were terrified. "It's a ghost, "they said and cried out in fear. But Jesus immediately said to them;" Take courage! It is l. don't be afraid" (Matt14:26-27) **I received an amusing e-mail on the subject "If heaven had voice mail…" that began with this question: have you ever wondered what it would be like if God decided to install voice mail? Imagine praying and hearing the following: Thank you for calling Heaven. For English, press 1. For Spanish, press 2. For all other languages, press O. Please select one of the following options:**

Press 1 for requests.

Press 2 for thanksgiving.

Press 3 for complains.

Press 4 for all other inquiries.

I am sorry: all of our angels and saints are busy helping other sinners right now. However, your prayer is important to us, and we will answer it in order it was received. Please stay on the line .1f you would like to speak to: <u>God, press 1. Jesus, press 2. Holy Spirit, press 3.</u> If you would like to hear king David sing a Psalm while you holding, press 4. To find a loved one that has been assigned to Heaven, press 5, then enter his or her social security number, followed by the "$" sign. (If you receive a

negative response, please hang up and try area code 666). For reservations at Heaven, please enter J-O-H-N, followed by the numbers 3-1-6. For answers to nagging questions about dinosaurs, the age of earth, life on other planets, and where Noah's Ark is, please wait until you arrive. Our computers show that you have already prayed today. Please hang-up and try again tomorrow. The office is now closed for the weekend to observe a religious holiday. Please pray again on Monday after 9:30 am. If you are calling after hours and need emergency assistance, please contact your local Pastor. Thank you, and have a Heavenly day! Aren't you glad that God makes direct contact with his children when they pray, that believers have direct access to him and conversation with him is not through a local carrier, an answering machine, or a personal computer? Jesus response was instantaneous (v 27) in hearing the disciples cry and seeing their panic. His words calmed fears dispelled doubts and answered questions. Relief, assurance and help were at hand. Both Matthew (v 27) and Mark (6:50) used the word "immediately" to describe Jesus direct response to the disciples fear and both ascribe similar words from Jesus mouth: "Take courage! It is I. don't be afraid." Jesus voice was forceful, familiar and friendly. His words were inspiring, instructive and influential, and His presence cheered, calmed, and comforted them. The disciples had no reason to fear when Jesus was nearby, with them and for them. It's been said "Don't fear" is a terrible, meaningless and negative piece of advice. All the boating versions in Matthew, Mark, and John record Jesus revealing His identity- "It Is I"- before issuing his "fear not" command Matt15:27, Mark 6:50, John 6:20) Jesus had never stopped with the word s "fear not" in all his words and ministry a positive command was always attached Jesus commission to Peter was, "Don't be afraid: Jesus did not promised the wind and the waves would subside or stop in our walking with him or to him. The only immediate promise in the passage is assured presence and helping hand (vv22, 27, 31) Testing the waters was a foolish idea, bad experiment and stubborn, reckless and childish desire that God permitted, not commanded. Jesus desire for his disciples is to walk by faith, not walk on water. Jesus rebuked Peter for his rapid forgetfulness, shallow understanding and hardened hearts even after Jesus had fed five thousand men, as interpreted by(Mark 6:52) Fear is costly , chronic and crippling disease. Some fear of failure, others of reprisal and many fear act. People with no heart , help or hope have reason to fear, but in Christ we have the promise, the ability and the backing to combat, contain and conquer fear (Romans 8:38-39) Someone once said, Sometimes the Lord calms the storm . Sometimes he lets the storm rage and calms his child." Fear is a test and not a trap. Jesus does not allow things to happen for the sake of thrilling, teasing, or tempting his children, but use it as an opportunity to deepen and deliver them. Are you walking by faith or by sight? Do you trust your experience or His expertise? Have you called out for his presence, fixed your eyes on him and hold on to his hand for your dear life when all else fails, blurs and changes... Then those who were in the boat worshiped him, saying, **"Truly you are the Son of God" (Matthew 14:28-33)**

ELDER TREMELL J. COLLINS
"A Storm IN A Tea Cup"

A JOURNEY WAS MADE
THE PRESSURE'S OFF

A journey was made a man who heard the Lord say to him "leave…" and so Abram set out as the Lord had bidden him because men of faith in Israel in every generation believed in this God. Who comes, who calls, and who promises. Briefly and without comment Abram's response to God's call and promise is noted he set out as the Lord had bidden him no attempt is made to explain or to justify this breaking of family ties. It is an example of that obedient faith which is one of the marks of Abram's Life. The descent to Egypt there came a famine in the land, so severe that Abram went down to Egypt he said to his wife Sarah I know very well that you are beautiful women and that when the Egyptians see you they will say she is his wife then they will kill me but let you live Tell them that you are my sister so that all may go well with me because of you and my life may be spared on your account. Interestingly this picture of Abram the man of faith in links together to sections in both of which Abram expresses doubts Lord God what canst thou give me? Verse 2 0 Lord God how can I be sure? Verse 8 such is not the opposite of faith. It is possible to trust God and yet live with very real uncertainties as to how God's purposes and promises are going to be fulfilled. The Old Testament gives us many such expressions of doubt set within the context of faith, not least in the Psalms see for example Psalms (22 and 73). The El-Rol means the God of vision or the God who sees me. Abraham kept hope aglow amid many years of heartaches and uncertainty. William F. Lynch images of hope when a moment comes which is impossible we can at least wait for the emergence of a larger moment and a larger time (pg29) we must learn to liberate hope and at the same time acknowledge and assert it. Hope is truly inside of us but hope is an interior sense that helps on the outside of us. (pg.31). "And what is Faith" The answer is "Faith gives substance to our hopes and makes us certain of realties we do not see" Heb 11:1 NEB) Abraham was subjected to three precarious and uncertain adventures in hope. First a journey to a New land, not knowing where it was. Next a long and perplexing deferment of the birth of his son of promise Isaac, and finally Isaac's release after Abraham took him to be sacrificed as a burnt offering never once doubted God Abraham responded through every trail with an incredible power to believe. Abraham walked by Faith and not by sight. Walking by faith is not the most natural thing on earth. Like any exercise, exercising our faith is easier said than done. No one is ever quite ready intellectually, emotionally or spiritually for God's ways, life's lessons, or unexpected turns. Abraham traveled a long way from his native Ur to Canaan. Along the road his farther died. The Promised Land was not a bed of roses, by any means. Abraham strayed into Egypt When a famine struck, separated from lot as their fortunes grew, took a concubine at his wife's insistence, and had a son with Sarah but also witnessed the departure of Ishmael, and his other son. However, whenever Abraham stumbled, slipped or stalled, faith rescued him, pulled him out, and put him back on his feet. A man of faith is not perfect in faith but persistent in faith. Abraham's triumph over his shortcomings, mistakes, weaknesses, blunders, and faults was nothing short of a miracle. He eventually overcame his inadequacies, suspicions, and fears and transformed himself into a giant man of faith. This world is not my home, I'm just passing through. "Say that man. Psalms 39:6 says, man is a mere phantom as we go to and from: He bustles about, but only in vain: he heaps up wealth, not knowing who will get it." People are like grass (Isa 40:7) and grasshoppers (Isa 40:22) here today and gone tomorrow. There is nine things Abraham leaves us with. I. Determine your present position 2. Be specific about what you want. 3. Look for the promise4. Ask God to help you 5. Identify the barriers 6. Create a step by step plan. 7. Be patient and persistent "These things I plan won't happen right away. Slowly, steadily, surely, the time approaches when the vision will be fulfilled. If it seems slow, do not despair, for these things will sure come to pass. Just be patient! They will not be overdue a single day!" Habakkuk 2:3 (LB). What the point? If you are going to really reach your goal in life, sometimes you have to delay gratification. You have to do the tough things instead of the fun things, the right things instead of the pleasurable thing. The pressure's off...

(GENESIS 24: 1-8 READ)

HEARTSHIFT

A heart shift is the conviction that we've on the wrong road and need of making a turn back to better, health, stronger relationship or a deeper faith...

Definition of what is meant by 2 degree changes once we've made a heart shift

A 2 degree change is taking the smallest of positive step, action, or corrections to begin, sustain, or move us towards a needed change...

Dance steps of Effective communication

1. Rule #1 Speak I statement not you! -Cause defense
2. Rule #2 Describe only feelings and needs using I statements this keeps the conflict from escalating out of control

LUV — Talk is not **Rocket science** it is a for door way of conflict L. U. V. is an Acronym for

Listen Understand and Validate

Negative feelings pocket deep or wells of anger if were still tied up in knots from lack of forgiveness we got to go to God in Prayer!

The Four Keys of Empathetic listening

1. Listen with an attitude of understanding (not judgment).
2. Withhold judgment on your spouse's ideas.
3. Affirm your spouse, even when you disagree with his or her ideas.
4. Share your own ideas only when your spouse feels understood.

"Taken from Gary Chapman's book The Four Seasons of Marriage

Which Season of Marriage are you in?"

Notes by ELDER TREMELL J. COLLINS

How Do You Get From A Desperate Situation To Your Intended Destination? by ELDER TREMELL J. COLLINS

FROM DESPERATION TO DESTINATION
EXODUS 14:10-15

Have you ever found yourself in a desperate situation...? Perhaps you've found yourself surrounded by people that didn't mean you any good... Perhaps you've found yourself overwhelmed with financial stress and strain... Perhaps you've found yourself going through some type of personal problem within your family life that has caused you to find yourself trapped in the difficulty and dilemma of desperation...? Have you gotten to a point in life where it seems as if the enemy has kept you from the destiny that God has ordained for you...? Have you gotten to the point where you're just about ready to give up...? Does it seems like your gumption is gone... Your hope has been halted... Your faith has faltered. And your victory has vanished...? Our text here shows us that this is indeed the situation with Israel... For they are indeed caught up in a desperate situation... They're caught... Between a rock and a hard place...!

Likewise I have discovered in this life that just as it was with the Israelites in times past, that many of us have been enslaved and engulfed by the enemy...! Some have been overcome and overwhelmed by the devil and his henchmen... Our "Modern Day Pharaoh" has literally withdrawn us from our destiny and has taken us out of position to move and operate according to the plan that God has destined for our lives...! Pharaoh has convinced us to identify ourselves as property and not people... Pharaoh has given us false definitions of who we are... Where we have come from and what contributions we have made to civilization.... He's got us in such a state, that we literally have become frozen in our tracks with fear (V10-11)...!

And so here we are today... Stuck on the banks of the Red Sea...Stuck on the edge of our very existence... With desperation surrounding us... And destiny lying before us, and... Pharaoh and his army closing in from behind...! We stand here stuck... Crying for help.. We desperately want to reach the destiny that God has prepared for us but we're stuck...! Frozen with fear and disabled by doubt... We're bound..

Financially bound...
Emotionally bound...
Spiritually bound...

And because of our bondage, we're stuck standing at the Red Sea of decision.... (Problem) You're just standing there doing nothing... You're can't turn around because if you do, Pharaoh (your past...) will overtake you... you're scared to go forward because before you lies the Red Sea (your destiny...) and reaching for your destiny requires you take a risk...

But if you're going to move from the banks of the sea to the Land of Promise... If you're going to move from a desperation to destiny, it's going to take some effort on your part...! There are going to be some prerequisites that must be met... If you're going to reach your destiny... If you plan to move from desperation to destiny, you've got to...

I. LET GO OF THE PAST (v 12)

The problem was they became accustomed to slavery... And comfortable in it...! They thought it better to stay in Egypt as slaves... (Look @ what they said, Deal w/ it)... We get in our comfort zone and don't want to change... It's funny how we are constantly living in the past... It's funny how we concentrate on how things used to be, what we used to have.. What we used to do... There's nothing wrong with memories... It's good to reminisce, but I want to let you know that you can't move forward by living in the past...We can never move forward, if we keep looking backwards...The Lord has been constantly proving Himself to us, taking us through dangers seen and unseen. Yet every' time He tries to take us to the next level, we stand there looking over our shoulder in retrospect, mulling over the past...! Israel was so paralyzed with fear that they were willing to give up and settle for a life of despondency and hopelessness...!

So many times we give up and settle for anything instead of receiving all that God has for us... We blame it on past failures... Past heartaches... Past bitter experiences... But if you're going to move to your destiny, you've got to Let Go of the Past...! We've got to stop allowing the enemy to convince us to return to the things that God has already brought us out of...! (Song: "Bag Lady...") Deals with women not being able to move forward because they're still holding on to their past... She encourages them to, "Pack light... One day all 'dem bags 'gon get in your way..."

I stopped by to tell you that you need to drop the excess bags... Because if you keep on carrying them around, they will derail and deter you from reaching your destiny in the things of God...! (Real problem, real reason you're still carrying that junk...) Although God has delivered us from all kinds of bondage, but we really haven't come out of them...! God has brought you out of_____, but you still can't progress because although He's brought you out of it, you haven't brought it out of you!!! (You missed it...!)

God has delivered you from...
That trifling brother, but...!
That gossiping tongue, but...!
Lazy, do-nothing attitude, but...!

Why...? Because your mind has not accepted the fact that God has brought you out... So you continue to long for what you left in Egypt, and until you change your thinking...Until you change your mindset...Until you let go of the past... You'll never be able to enter to reach your destiny...!

The Word of God says that we have to be transformed by the renewing of our mind...! It's only by our renewed thinking that we can move from desperation to our destiny that God has called us to have...! (Tell somebody) "Let Go Of The Past...!" Secondly, if you're going reach your destiny, you've got to...

II. LOOK TO YOUR FAITH (v 13-14)

(V13) Don't be afraid... Don't allow the enemy to keep you in the confinement of fear... For fear is NOT of the Lord... In fact fear is OPPOSITE of faith...! F.E.A.R. is nothing more than False Evidence Appearing Real...! It's a trick that the enemy will use to keep you entangled and entrapped in his snare...! (It's a mind thing...) But Timothy lets us know that "God has not given us the spirit of fear..." So if you're operating in fear, you're not operating in the power of the Lord...! In spite of what it looks like...In spite of what's coming behind you.... No matter how Pharaoh tries to plant the device of fear in your spirit, just stand boldly on God's Promises... Stand boldly on God's Word... And Look to Your Faith...!

(Problem) Israel didn't believe that God would bring them out...! In spite of all that He'd done for them... In spite of all the plagues that He cast upon the Egyptians... They didn't believe that God would see them through...!

In spite of all God's done for us... In spite of the dangers He's seen us through... We've got to learn how to Look To Our Faith...! Because when you look to your faith you'll be able to stand still...!

The text says, "Stand still, and see the salvation of the Lord...!" "Stand Still..." means literally, relax and take your hands off... In other words, be still and watch God move...! We've got to learn how to let the Lord fight our battles...We've got to allow God to move in His own time...! So many times we want to put God on our own schedule... We want Him to move at our every beck and call... But you need to learn how to wait on God...!

(Isaiah 40:31...) (Secret) With waiting... Comes renewal... With waiting... Comes renewed faith... With waiting... Comes renewed strength... With waiting... Comes renewed zeal... (Point) When we learn how to look to our faith and depend on the Lord, God will begin to move on our behalf... He'll begin to work in the midst of our circumstances He'll begin to operate in our favor... In other words, if we just trust in Him, and look to our faith... He'll begin to strengthen our hearts... He'll begin to strengthen our mind, will, and emotions... So that we'll become responsive to His commands... We'll simply stand still and trust in His Word...! We'll simply "Stand still... And see the salvation of the Lord...!"

(Understand this concept of waiting...) We'll be able to "Stand Still..." And let God do what He does best...!

"Stand Still..." And watch God move on your behalf... "Stand Still..." And Look to your Faith...! (Title) Just "Stand Still..." There's a blessing in waiting...! Just ask Jehoshaphat (2 Chron 20:17)... "There's no need for you to fight... Stand Still... Be Still... And see the salvation of the Lord...!" He's telling us in Psalms 46: 10, "Be still and know...! I've brought you out in times past... I've led you by clouds in the day, by fire in the night.... I gave fed you when you were hungry, drink when you were thirsty..." (Make it personal...) I can be still because:

He's been my burden sharer...
My heavy load bearer...
He's brought me through storm, rain, sickness and pain...
He's brought me up...
Out of a horrible pit...
Out of the miry clay...
And set my feet upon a rock...

(Trying to say...) If you want to make it through in a desperate situation... Just Let Go Of Your Past...! Look To Your Faith...! And finally you've got to...

III. LAUNCH FORWARD! (v 15)

If you want reach your destiny... If you want to attain and achieve all that God has for you, you've got to launch forward... Into Kingdom Principles... For just as Jesus told the disciples in Luke 5:4 to "Launch out into the deep and lay down your nets for a catch..." I hear the Lord telling us we've got to launch out into the sea of life... And lay down our nets.... Lay down your mindset... Lay down your way of thinking... Lay down your attitude and perception of things... And receive your catch...! Receive your deliverance from the hand of Pharaoh... But most of all... You've got to lay down your net that's filled with ways of the world... And receive your Destiny...! You've got to launch forward...! The text says...(v 15) We've got to learn how to go forward in the things of God... If you really want to go forward, you've got to learn how to move at His command...Learn how to Go forward in His...

I. Presence: (David & Goliath, 3 Hebrew Boys)
II. Power: (2 Tim 4:13)
III. Promise: (Josh 1:15, Matt 28:20)

Just launch forward... No matter what comes your way...! It's not that God doesn't want to move, but He's waiting for you to move in faith...!

THE LANDMINES OF LIFE

There have been plenty of times in our lives where we are discouraged. We get distressed for various reasons. Sometimes it is because we are under attack. Other times it is because we cause trouble for ourselves. When we put too much trust in others, we can very easily be let down. We have received a promise from God that he is not a man and he can never lie. Family and friends are human: they have problems and challenges just like we do. If we depend on them for everything we get let down when they go through a challenges and aren't there to save us. Overtake- Overwhelm/ without effort/ /without casualty/ without fail. Conquer-requires energy/ human power and logic/ requires battle/ casualties. Steal- to take undercover/ without being noticed/ with the intent to not be found out recover- to take without force as a gift/ reward given by a supernatural authority. What causes discouragement? #1Cause fatigue when you're physically or emotionally exhausted, you're a prime candidate to be infected with discouragement. Your defenses are lower and things can seem bleaker than they really are. This often occurs when your half way through a major project and you get tired. #2Cause Frustration When unfinished tasks piles up, it natural to feel overwhelmed. And when trivial matters or the unexpected interrupt you and prevent you from accomplishing what you really need to do, your frustration can easily produce discouragement. #3 causes Failure- sometimes your best laid out plans fall apart the project collapses the deal falls through no one shows up to the event. How do you react? Do you give into self-pity? Do you blame others? As one man said, "just when I think I can makes ends meet somebody moves the ends! That's discouraging!"

#4 Cause-Fear — fear is behind more discouragement than we'd like to admit. The fear of criticism (What will they think ?) the fear of responsibility (what if I can't handle this ?) and fear of failure (what if I blow it) can cause a major onset of the blues. What's the cure for discouragement. There is a story in the bible about a guy named Nehemiah mobilized the residents of

Jerusalem to build a wall around the entire city. Half way through the project, the citizens became discouraged and wanted to give up because of the four causes I've given. Here what Nehemiah taught about defeating discouragement (Nehemiah 4):

Rest your body — if you need a break take one! You'll be more effective when you return work. If you're burning the candle at both ends, you're not as bright as you think! (Psalms 116:7)

Reorganize your life- Discouragement doesn't necessary mean you are doing wrong thing. It may just be that you are doing the right thing in the wrong way. Try a new approach. Shake things up a little.

Remember God will help you — Just ask him. He can give you new energy. There's incredible motivating power in faith. (Psalms 42:11; 3 John 2). Don't let joy stealer steal your joy God is our presence help in a time of need. We have got to recognize the presence of God in a new way & manner.

Resist the Discouragement- Fight back! Discouragement is a choice. If you feel discouraged, it's because you've chosen to feel that way. No one is forcing you to feel bad. Hang on! Do what's right in spite of your feelings. No feeling lasts forever. (Deut. 28: 10-14)

Be Presences driven with God... Don't surrender to your circumstances stand up and fight! We win when we resist if we fail to resist we will follow a fake that is beyond horror... There is power in his presences no matter how confused and confusing a situation is the presence of God will bring order into that situation so we should carry the fire about anywhere we go knowing God is able.

"A TEA BAG ROMANS 8:28"

The Apostle Paul said in Romans 8:28: "And we know that all things work together for the good to them that love God, and to them who are called according to his purpose."

This is one of the most blessed promises that the bible record, but many of us do not believe it. We don't believe God is behind everything, working it out for our good. Sometimes we go through hard times, and we cannot understand why the troubles come our way. But we need to realize and look up into the loving eyes of God and say... "Lord I put my trust in thee." Even thou ...I don't know why troubles comes upon me. Even thou... I don't know what tomorrow may bring. But I do know that.. "You're going to work it out for my good. Our text does not say that all things will work out for all people. But it does say to those who love God. AII things work out for good. The promise today is God Children those who love the lord and those called according to his purpose. If you're living in unrepeated sin you cannot say, Things are being worked out for your good. Things don't work for your good on promise of this word. Unless you are and living for the lord. A born again Christian can stand at the casket of a loved one and say good-bye and know that the words of our text are true." All things work for the good of them that love the lord. In our hour s of deepest sorrow and hardest of trials and greatest of temptations, We can know these words are true. Your enemies may assail. You but God has it all. Your friends may desert. You, but God has it all worked out. The mysteries of life may engulf you. But God has it all worked out. Poverty may threaten you. God has it all worked out. Satan may buffet you and demons beset you. But God has it all worked out. But when you feel like God has turned his back against you he's still there working things out for you! When you feel that God's face is hidden against you. He still busy working things out for you! If you hold out until tomorrow everything will be alright. There is a silver lining behind every dark cloud. "If you just hold out "until tomorrow.. You see the sunshine peeping through dark clouds, because your help is on the way. A diamond must be cut to bring out the beauty.. Gold must be refined to bring out its purity. A vine must be pruned to bear fruit.

The process may seem hard, but we ought to always say in our hearts: Have thine own way lord have thine own way! Thou are the potter, I am the clay mold me after thy will. While I am waiting, yielded and still.

Yes God will work it out and help is on the way.

SLAYING YOUR GAINTS: 5 STAGES

ELDER TREMELL J. COLLINS

"A TEA BAG IN A HOT WATER WORLD"

1 SAMUEL 17; 3-17

WE will consider a famous story this night from the valley of death and pain. A valley suggests lowliness, fertility, and fruitfulness- born out of struggle. And that is what we have1 Samuel 17

David was on the lord side- and was in trouble spot. He didn't start the trouble .but neither did he shrink from it. He dealt with it, & and overcame the adversity.

In this heroic story, the enemy is doing the boasting and threatening. But God's man does not back down. He treated Goliath the way we need to treat temptation. He didn't entertain Goliath, didn't give in to him, and didn't try to ignore him. He defeated him ! And we see it happening in five steps.

1. Trained kicking without his contact lenses

The fist principle is that victories are first won not on the playing field but in the training room.

In Paul's words "everyone who competes in the games goes into strict training. They do it to get a crown that will not last; but we do it to get a crown that will last forever. Therefore I do not run like a man running aimlessly; I do not fight like a man beating the air, air no I beat my body and make it my slave so that after I have preached to others ,l myself will not be disqualified for the prize... "IN other word* the final victory demands more than determination. It requires discipline. Former Michigan State football coach Duffy Daugherty tells a great story about a winning field goal kicked by a young man name Dave Kaiser against UCLA many years ago. The game was Los Angeles and the field goal gave Michigan a 17-14 victory. As Dave Kaiser came back to the bench to meet the roaring enthusiasm of his teammates, Coach Daugherty said;" nice going, Dave, but I notice you didn't watch the ball after you kick it. How come? Kaiser replied, you're right coach I didn't watch the ball. I was watching the referee to see how he would call it. You see I forgot my contact Lenses. They are back at the hotel. I couldn't even see the goal post. Daugherty was shocked and at first very angry that Kaiser had not told him about his contact lenses. But after he thought it over he changed his mind entirely. Why shouldn't Kaiser kick without his contact lenses? Kaiser was disciplined kicker and practiced for long hours. He knew well the angel and the distance to the goal even though he could not see it. The whole process of kicking the ball was programmed into his body and mind by the ongoing discipline of daily practice. In that moment, when the ball went through the goal posts, discipline paid off. Think of this moment; we see no military career for David prior to this. We see a young man tending sheep and spending a lot of time worshiping God. So where was his training? That was his training! Spending time with God and living a normal life. And through he probably didn't know it God was fitting David for service. David grew to know God secretly, worship him privately; Now God could reward him openly. You never really know what kind of emergency you can handle, after you've spent quality time with God. The lord had been preparing David to win all along. He already made him able to fight against a loin and a bear .So while the soldiers out there trembled, David surprised them all by going out and saying, "Hey — how dare this man curse God. You see the frightened solders had been trained in warfare. But not handling something as big as Goliath. For that you need God. And David had Godly training."

2. Tripped-up

Notice it was David's own brother who tried to stop him from going out to get goliath. It's easy for us today to look back and say, sure God could use a shepherd to kill a giant But his own brothers were close to the situation. It's been harder to have faith up close. When King Saul finally gave in to letting David go fight; he tried to help out by piling on armor on David. But it didn't help... It was like tossing of his trust in the world and the world's tools.

3. Taunted

Getting past his own king and brothers should have been enough.

Getting past his inner own feelings of reservation; but here was the moment of truth

His Giant

His mountain

His Trail

His crisis

Speaking out to him and taunting him! There are things you face in life, either publicly or privately, that rise up like mountains before they make you feel small. When Goliath laughed and cursed David, David could have retreated right then. And nobody would have blamed him. Whatever you might be facing today —as you feel the ground shaking beneath you —look at what David did! He stood his ground!

4. Trusting

To trust God in the face of Goliath:

A Giant that you can see with your eyes, hear with your ears;
To trust a God you can't see at a time like that? The world called it crazy. The world still does.

Imagine little you running up to the face a giant who had been able to terrify a whole nation.

These 5 smooth stones. Let's let them represent 5 weapons of truth that can apply to David and to you:

Christ Is- Isa.51; confidence.

Christ Can-Luke 11:22 can conquer. Christ Has-mark 16:17 all power.

Christ Will-1st John5:4-5 will give us victory.

Christ Does-Rev-12:11 he causes us to overcome.

5. Spiritual Growth

We are growing spiritually when:

- We are experiencing an increasing awareness of his presence

- We are jealously guard our private time of prayer and bible reading

- We view service for him as high honor and not a burden

- Our response to sin is quick and follow by genuine repentance

- We see trails and temptations as opportunities for growth

- We sense our faith is growing stronger when our faith level rises or when it takes more to "ruffle" us

- Our spiritual battles are becoming more fierce and yet we still rejoice

- We view everything that comes our way as being from God (Romans 8:28?)

Our deliverer is Jesus mighty to save. And he can give you victory over anything that hindered your walk with God: a bad habit, bad memory, a tough situation.

SLAYING YOUR GAINTS: 5 STAGES

ELDER TREMELLJ. COLLINS

"A TEA BAG IN A HOT WATER WORLD"

1 SAMUEL 17; 3-17

WE will consider a famous story this night from the valley of death and pain. A valley suggests lowliness, fertility, and fruitfulness- born out of struggle. And that is what we have 1 Samuel 17

David was on the lord side- and was in trouble spot. He didn't start the trouble .but neither did he shrink from it. He dealt with it, & and overcame the adversity. In this heroic story, the enemy is doing the boasting and threatening. But God's man does not back down. He treated Goliath the way we need to treat temptation. He didn't entertain Goliath, didn't give in to him, and didn't try to ignore him. He defeated him! And we see it happening in five steps.

1. Trained kicking without his contact; lenses

The fist principle is that victories are first won not on the playing field but in the training room.

In Paul's words "everyone who competes in the games goes into strict training. They do it to get a crown that will not last; but we do it to get a crown that will last forever. Therefore I do not run like a man running aimlessly; I do not fight like a man beating the air, air no I beat my body and make it my slave so that after I have preached to others, I myself will not be disqualified for the prize... "IN other words, the final victory demands more than determination. It requires discipline. Former Michigan State football coach Duffy Daugherty tells a great story about a winning field goal kicked by a young man name Dave Kaiser against UCLA many years ago. The game was Los Angeles and the field goal gave Michigan a 17-14 victory. As Dave Kaiser came back to the bench to meet the roaring enthusiasm of his teammates, Coach Daugherty said;" nice going, Dave, but I notice you didn't watch the ball after you kick it. How come? Kaiser replied, you're right coach I didn't watch the ball. I was watching the referee to see how he would call it. You see I forgot my contact Lenses. They are back at the hotel. I couldn't even see the goal post. Daugherty was shocked and at first very angry that Kaiser had not told him about his contact lenses. But after he thought it over he changed his mind entirely. Why shouldn't Kaiser kick without his contact lenses? Kaiser was disciplined kicker and practiced for long hours. He knew well the angel and the distance to the goal even though he could not see it. The whole process of kicking the ball was programmed into his body and mind by the ongoing discipline of daily practice. In that moment, when the ball went through the goal posts, discipline paid off. Think of this moment; we see no military career for David prior to this. We see a young man tending sheep and spending a lot of time worshiping God. So where was his. training? That was his training! Spending time with God and living a normal life. And through he probably didn't know it God was fitting David for service. David grew to know God secretly, worship him privately; Now God could reward him openly. You never really know what kind of emergency you can handle, after you've spent quality time with God. The lord had been preparing David to win all along. He already made him able to fight against a loin and a bear .So while the soldiers out there trembled, David surprised them all by going out and saying, "Hey —how dare this man curse God. You see the frightened solders had been trained in warfare. But not handling something as big as Goliath. For that you need God. And David had Godly training."

2. Tripped- up

Notice it was David's own brother who tried to stop him from going out to get goliath. It is easy for us today to look back and say, sure God could use a shepherd to kill a giant But his own brothers were close to the situation. It's been harder to have faith close. When King Saul finally gave in to letting David go fight; he tried to help out by piling on armor on David. But it didn't help... It was like tossing of his trust in the world and the world's tools.

3. Taunted

Getting past his own king and brothers should have been enough.

Getting past his inner own feelings of reservation; but here was the moment of truth

His Giant

His mountain

His Trail

His crisis

Speaking out to him and taunting him! There are things you face in life, either publicly or privately, that rise up like mountains before they make you feel small. When Goliath laughed and cursed David, David could have retreated right then. And nobody would have blamed him. Whatever you might be facing today —as you feel the ground shaking beneath you —look at what David did! He stood his ground!

4. Trusting

To trust God in the face of Goliath:

A Giant that you can see with your eyes, hear with your ears;

To trust a God you can't see at a time like that? The world called it crazy. The world still does.

Imagine little you running up to the face a giant who had been able to terrify a whole nation.

These 5 smooth stones. Let's let them represent 5 weapons of truth that can apply to David and to you:

Christ Is- Isa.51; confidence.

Christ Can-Luke 11:22 can conquer.

Christ Has-mark 16:17 all power.

Christ Will-ISt John5:4-5 will give us victory.

Christ Does-Rev-12:11 he causes us to overcome.

5. Spiritual Growth

We are growing spiritually when:

- We are experiencing an increasing awareness of his presence

- We are jealously guard our private time of prayer and bible reading

- We view service for him as high honor and not a burden

- Our response to sin is quick and follow by genuine repentance

- We see trails and temptations as opportunities for growth

- We sense our faith is growing stronger when our faith level rises or when it takes more to "ruffle" us

- Our spiritual battles are becoming more fierce and yet we still rejoice

- We view everything that comes our way as being from God (Romans 8:28?)

Our deliverer is Jesus mighty to save. And he can give you victory over anything that hindered your walk with God: a bad habit, bad memory, a tough situation.

A TEA BAG IN
A HOT WATER
WORLD

ACKNOWLEDGEMENTS:

I acknowledge those individuals who have given me suggestions and thoughts and helped me compile and put together this book. Bobby jean Williams, Bob Peterson, Michelle Vestal, Ben Maxwell, to all my Sons Tyrelle, Tremell Jr, Travon and all family members I love you all. Those who criticized mocked and did not believe in the book I thank you. You kept me on my Knees you kept me desperate for God to do the Impossible you kept me Determined to do thus said The Lord... Grateful Acknowledgements is given to numerous contributions throughout my life and Ministry mentioned and UN mentioned who have poured into me shared me, and believed in the call of God on my life...

TEA BAG IN A HOT WATER WORLD

TEA BAG IN A HOT WATER WORLD

USING EXAMPLES FROM THE
BIBLE COMTEMPORARY STORIES
ANDEXPERIENCES FROM HIS OWN
LIFE TREMELL COLLINS SR POINTS
THE WAY TO A DEEPER RICHER
LIFE HELPEING YOU TAKE HOLD OF
EVERTHING GOD WANTS TO GIVE

A TEA BAG IN A HOT WATER WORLD

WRITTEN BY TREMELL J. COLLINS SR.

What Did You Expect? by
ELDER TREMELL J COLLINS

Psalms 62: 5-62:7

Psalm 62:5-7

"[5] My soul, wait silently for God alone, for my expectation [is] from Him. [6] He only [is] my rock and my salvation; [He is] my defense; I shall not be moved. [7] In God [is] my salvation and my glory; the rock of my strength, [And] my refuge, [is] in God". [NKJV]

Are you expecting today? Are you anticipating something from the Lord? I'm here today to let you know that if you are expecting something — you will receive it. But if you are expecting nothing.... You will receive it! If you expect something today — I hope that your expectation comes from the Lord Himself!

It is time that the Church of the Living God began to ELEVATE THEIR EXPECTATIONS!

What is it that you are expecting today? Or ARE you expecting nothing? Either way, you can have what you expect!

Just after the Apostle Paul was imprisoned for preaching the Gospel - and just as he was facing impending death for doing so - he wrote a letter to the church of Philippi and said this:

"[19] ...For I know that this will turn out for my deliverance through your prayer and the supply of the Spirit of Jesus Christ, [20] according to my earnest expectation and hope that in nothing I shall be ashamed, but with all boldness, as always, so now also Christ will be magnified in my body, whether by life or by death. [21] For to me, to live [is] Christ, and to die [is] gain." Philippians 1:19-21 [NKJV]

Notice what he says there — "I know this will turn out (or turn around) for my deliverance through your prayers & through the supply of the Spirit of God-according to my earnest expectation!" His expectation was deliverance!

The word 'deliverance' Paul uses there is debated often. And I'm not sure why because all you have to do is go to the original Greek text. Some say Paul was confident that God would keep him healthy enough to live out the remainder of his years in prison — healthy - but in prison. That's ridiculous — because that would imply God only gets 1/2 the job done! The Greek text for the word 'deliverance' there that Paul used is translated as 'salvation.'

But that-to me — isn't even the real message of Paul's statement. To me it is what he says 'after' that. He said he knows he will be delivered (or saved) because of the Spirit in Him, because of the prayers of the believers... AND... because (or according TO) his earnest expectation and hope!

Walking in the Spirit is enough for certain. The intercession of the saints on your behalf is quite powerful, to say the least. But when you add those 2 things along WITH earnest expectation.... You cannot lose!

Remember our text: "...my expectation is from God!" That's powerful!

When you translate that phrase "earnest expectation" out of the Greek — it means something quite striking. It means to watch with your head outstretched; to direct attention to something; to wait in suspense for something. But for the Greek words used here — there is a prefix which implicates a plural expectation — in other words — and ongoing, constant, persistent expectation.

When a woman is with child we say she is 'expecting.' And as the time gets closer to her due date — her expectation becomes more persistent and grows in intensity.

Just this past week we heard the news of the 5.9 earthquake that shook parts of the East Coast, primarily in the Washington, DC area. Everyone has been watching closely also for a potential hurricane to hit the East Coast as well. First of all, I find it rather interesting that these two potentially life-altering events are hitting close to DC. There's something spiritually significant to that I'm sure — I've not figured it out yet —what that is. But, nonetheless, two events that could both bring potential damage. And the first passage of Scripture I thought of this week was Romans 8:19.

"For the earnest expectation of the creation eagerly waits for the revealing of the sons of God." Romans 8:19 [NKJV]

And then skip to verse 22: "For we know that the whole creation groans and labors with birth pangs together until now." Romans 8:22

The earth itself is just like that woman in her third trimester. When it's time to groan with labor pains. The earth is groaning as we speak — waiting eagerly with earnest expectation for the sons of God to be revealed!

What does that mean? That means that even the very universe — all of creation itself has been given an earnest expectation from God — that one day we which are called the Elect will rule and reign over this earth as a new earth, remodeled, refurbished by the power of God Himself! We will rule as kings, as the sons & daughters of the Creator Himself! Even the EARTH is moving under our feet in anticipation! Even the sky is falling before our very eyes in earnest expectation of this great glorious day!

IF the EARTH can anticipate what God has in store — why not you?

The word translated "eager expectation" is a fascinating one in Greek that could literally be pulled apart to mean "from-head-watch."

It paints the picture of a person straining his head forward to watch with eager anticipation. It's what reminded me of the story of Zacchaeus craning his neck to see over the crowd.

The Apostle Paul said — my earnest expectation is that this thing will turn around for me! Let's look at the dictionary definitions of these two words — shall we?

ear•nest adjective
1. serious in intention, purpose, or effort; sincerely zealous.
2. showing depth and sincerity of feeling.
3. seriously important; demanding or receiving serious attention.

ex•pec•ta•tion noun
1. the act or the state of expecting.
2. the act or state of looking forward or anticipating.
3. an expectant mental attitude.
4. something expected; a thing looked forward to.

ex•pect verb (used with object)
1. to look forward to; regard as likely to

       happen; anticipate the occurrence or the coming of.
2. to look for with reason or justification.

It sounds a lot like operating in faith, doesn't it?

The Psalmist said: "In the morning, LORD, you hear my voice; in the morning I lay my requests before you and wait expectantly." Psalm 5:3 [NIV]

Why can we wait 'expectantly?' Because our expectation is FROM HIM!

ILL: A man approached a little league baseball game one afternoon. He asked a boy in the dugout what the score was. The boy responded, "Eighteen to nothing-we're behind." "Boy," the man said, "I'll bet you're discouraged."

"Why should I be discouraged?" replied the little boy. "We haven't even gotten up to bat yet!

Now that's expectation!
What do you expect? Every morning when you get up, you expect something. And the Bible teaches us that expectancy has so much to do with our faith. Faith is more than hoping, faith is more than wishing, faith is more than desire, faith is certainly not pretending, it is not psyching yourself up psychologically, faith is living in positive expectation. Faith is expecting the best. Faith is an attitude of confidence. When David went out to

fight Goliath, he said this is what I am going to do by the power of God. There was not an "if" not a "but" not an "and". David went out expecting victory, expecting to defeat the giant and that is exactly what happened.

Jesus said to two blind men, according to your faith so be it unto you. So what do you expect today? Those blind men expected Jesus to heal them and Jesus stretched forth His hand and He healed them because that is what they expected. Whatever you expect to feel, that is what you are going to feel. Whatever you expect to happen that is usually what happens. Whatever you expect to achieve is what you achieve. So what you expect influences your happiness, influences your level of achievement, influences your power and your strength in the Lord. It is so basic to the Christian life to expect the best because what you get is what you expect.

You remember Job? Job's problem is the same problem a lot of us have so many times. Job focused on what he didn't want to happen rather than on what he did want to happen. Job said the thing that I feared has come upon me. And I know so many people who just like that lady who said, when I feel good I feel bad because I know pretty soon I will feel bad again. They are focusing on what they don't want. I don't want my marriage to end in divorce. I don't want to be fired from my job; I don't want to fail in this task. And they set themselves up for failure. You give them a job to do and they say, well, preacher, I don't think I can do that job.

And then when they fail, they say I told you I didn't think I could do it. And you see, they are bestowing upon themselves self-fulfilling prophecy and they are not expecting the best.

In our text — the Psalmist declares "My expectation is from the Lord." Where is your expectation from? What do you expect today?

Teabag in A Hot Water World